LANGUAGE AND LIT

Dorothy S. Strickland
Celia Genishi and Donna E. A

ADVISORY BOARD: Richard Allington, Kathryn Au, Berni
Carole Edelsky, Shirley Brice Heath, Connie

M000307851

(continued)

For volumes in the NCRLL Collection (edited by JoBeth Allen and Donna E. Alvermann) and the Practitioners Bookshelf Series (edited by Celia Genishi and Donna E. Alvermann), as well as a complete list of titles in this series, please visit www.tcpress.com.

Urban Literacies
VALERIE KINLOCH, ED.

Bedtime Stories and Book Reports
CATHERINE COMPTON-LILLY & STUART GREENE, EDS.

Envisioning Knowledge
JUDITH A. LANGER

Envisioning Literature, Second Edition
JUDITH A. LANGER

Writing Assessment and the Revolution in
Digital Texts and Technologies
MICHAEL R. NEAL

Artifactual Literacies
KATE PAHL & JENNIFER ROWSELL

Educating Emergent Bilinguals
OFELIA GARCÍA & JO ANNE KLEIFGEN

(Re)Imagining Content-Area Literacy Instruction
RONI JO DRAPER, ED.

Change Is Gonna Come
PATRICIA A. EDWARDS, GWENDOLYN THOMPSON MCMILLON, &
JENNIFER D. TURNER

When Commas Meet Kryptonite
MICHAEL BITZ

Literacy Tools in the Classroom
RICHARD BEACH, GERALD CAMPANO, BRIAN EDMISTON,
& MELISSA BORGMANN

Harlem on Our Minds
VALERIE KINLOCH

Teaching the New Writing
ANNE HERRINGTON, KEVIN HODGSON, & CHARLES MORAN, EDS.

Critical Encounters in High School English, Second Edition
DEBORAH APPLEMAN

Children, Language, and Literacy
CELIA GENISHI & ANNE HAAS DYSON

Children's Language
JUDITH WELLS LINDFORS

"You Gotta BE the Book," Second Edition
JEFFREY D. WILHELM

No Quick Fix
RICHARD L. ALLINGTON & SEAN A. WALMSLEY, EDS.

Children's Literature and Learning
BARBARA A. LEHMAN

Storytime
LARWRENCE R. SIPE

Effective Instruction for Struggling Readers, K–6
BARBARA M. TAYLOR & JAMES E. YSSELDYKE, EDS.

The Effective Literacy Coach
ADRIAN RODGERS & EMILY M. RODGERS

Writing in Rhythm
MAISHA T. FISHER

Reading the Media
RENEE HOBBS

teaching**media***literacy*.com
RICHARD BEACH

What Was It Like?
LINDA J. RICE

Research on Composition
PETER SMAGORINSKY, ED.

The Vocabulary Book
MICHAEL F. GRAVES

Powerful Magic
NINA MIKKELSEN

New Literacies in Action
WILLIAM KIST

Teaching English Today
BARRIE R.C. BARRELL ET AL., EDS.

Bridging the Literacy Achievement Gap, 4–12
DOROTHY S. STRICKLAND & DONNA E. ALVERMANN, EDS.

Out of This World
HOLLY VIRGINIA BLACKFORD

Critical Passages
KRISTIN DOMBEK & SCOTT HERNDON

Making Race Visible
STUART GREENE & DAWN ABT-PERKINS, EDS.

The Child as Critic, Fourth Edition
GLENNA SLOAN

Room for Talk
REBEKAH FASSLER

Give Them Poetry!
GLENNA SLOAN

The Brothers and Sisters Learn to Write
ANNE HAAS DYSON

"Just Playing the Part"
CHRISTOPHER WORTHMAN

The Testing Trap
GEORGE HILLOCKS, JR.

Inquiry Into Meaning
EDWARD CHITTENDEN & TERRY SALINGER, WITH ANNE M. BUSSIS

"Why Don't They Learn English?"
LUCY TSE

Conversational Borderlands
BETSY RYMES

Inquiry-Based English Instruction
RICHARD BEACH & JAMIE MYERS

WRITING AND TEACHING TO CHANGE THE WORLD

Connecting with Our Most Vulnerable Students

Stephanie Jones

EDITOR

Foreword by Ann Lieberman

Teachers College, Columbia University
New York and London

NATIONAL WRITING PROJECT

National Writing Project
Berkeley, CA

Published simultaneously by Teachers College Press, 1234 Amsterdam Avenue, New York, NY 10027 and the National Writing Project, 2105 Bancroft Way, Berkeley, CA 94720-1042

The National Writing Project (NWP) is a nationwide network of educators working together to improve the teaching of writing in the nation's schools and in other settings. NWP provides high-quality professional development programs to teachers in a variety of disciplines and at all levels, from early childhood through university. Through its network of nearly 200 university-based sites, NWP develops the leadership, programs and research needed for teachers to help students become successful writers and learners.

The National Writing Project supported this teacher research project through a Teacher Inquiry Communities Network Minigrant.

Library of Congress Cataloging-in-Publication Data

Writing and teaching to change the world : connecting with our most vulnerable
    students / edited by Stephanie Jones.
        pages cm. — (Language and literacy series)
    ISBN 978-0-8077-5525-9 (pbk. : alk. paper) —
    ISBN 978-0-8077-7282-9 (ebook : alk. paper)
        1. Critical pedagogy. I. Jones, Stephanie, 1971–
    LC196.W75 2014
    370.11'5—dc23   2013045375

ISBN 978-0-8077-5525-9 (paper)
eISBN 978-0-8077-7282-9

Printed on acid-free paper
Manufactured in the United States of America

21 20 19 18 17 16 15 14   8 7 6 5 4 3 2 1

Contents

Foreword

I read *Writing and Teaching to Change the World* all in one day. It reminded me of my time teaching 6th grade as if it was yesterday, rather than over 40 years ago. I tried hard to connect with all kinds of students and was learning, struggling, and sometimes making it, all on the same day. As the writers describe so well in this book, it is not only *what* you teach, or even *how* you teach, but the *ways* you learn to connect with your students and the lives they live.

This book is a collection of stories from several different teachers who organize a teacher inquiry community (TIC) and decide to study one student in each of their classes who they think is vulnerable in some way. This TIC is part of the Red Clay Writing Project community. The book has three big ideas that bind together the individual stories which make this a powerful contribution to our understanding of the complexities of teaching: teachers' research, inquiry over time, and working together in a community.

These three ideas appear in each story as the relationship between the teacher and their vulnerable student emerges. Pressed with teaching to the curriculum, the teachers try mightily to figure out why their particular student does not connect to the work of the class and the assignments that are given. Why is this? What can I do to get closer to this student so I can understand how to get this student to engage? These are the questions as well as the written descriptions that the teachers bring to their TIC as they meet throughout the year. And it is here that each of the teachers begins to get ideas, insights, sensitivities, and different ways of thinking that move each teacher closer to working *with* rather than *on* the student who is the object of their research. Teachers learn to reveal their uncertainties as to what to do and are encouraged to push harder on the things that have been unknown to them in the past.

My favorite is the story of Mack as the teacher learns to *read the world* (before she *reads the word*). In Mack's case, the teacher learns to connect Mack's home life to school and in so doing helps Mack begin to engage in reading. He brings family pictures, talks about small moments in family history, and comes alive in the classroom. When he asks, "Can we write a book like this?" the teacher asks the students, and with a resounding "yes," she and the students get to work connecting their lives to their school through writing. Her TIC supports the teacher and her ideas and encourages a different way of thinking about connecting to one's students.

In the process we learn about how to listen to our students more carefully, continue to challenge our assumptions about teaching and learning, and let go of the control and the power we hold over students. In so doing, we learn more about the lives of our students, what they are experiencing and what pleases or disturbs them in their life. Instead of pushing difficult students away, we learn to sometimes take a jump in, close the distance, and engage in what can be thoughtful conversations.

What I love about this book is that it shows the deeply emotional side of teaching and puts it out there for us to use to become more sensitive to our students' lives, which often are so different from ours. Each of the chapters on these vulnerable students teaches us about ourselves as teachers even as the inquiry group opens teachers up to take risks, to become vulnerable, giving students more and different opportunities to connect teaching and curriculum to their lives.

Writing down our experiences with a focus on one child turns out to be an incredible opportunity to learn how to shake the stereotypes that are so easy to fall back on when we find ourselves frustrated with our students.

This is an important book for all teachers to read, from beginners to experienced practitioners. It provokes all of us as teachers to pay attention to the social and political contexts within which we work and consider what we often ignore—our students' lives outside of school.

—Ann Lieberman
senior scholar
Stanford University

Acknowledgments

We would like to thank the National Writing Project for supporting this Teacher Inquiry Community study, JoBeth Allen and Bob Fecho for their collaborative participation in this project, and all the members of the Red Clay Writing Project community and our students, whose voices are inherently diffracted through this text.

CHAPTER 1

Assembling a Critical Pedagogy

Stephanie Jones

What we learn *not* to see is shaped by fear, and . . . learning to see differently requires a willingness to live with new fears—what I call learning to inhabit a morally ambiguous self. As we learn to see differently . . . we may actually gain relief from the pain of separateness.

—Megan Boler, *Feeling Power: Emotions and Education*

Tears welled up.

A sob choked.

Laughter bellowed.

Smiles widened.

We sat together across a year listening to teachers reading their writing about the students for whom they were most concerned, and emotions ran high. Each teacher struggled with confusion about what to do next in the classroom as she forced herself to pay close attention to—to listen and hear and see—a student who was not "making it" in the school context. Pity, anger, powerlessness, surprise, affection, happiness, hope, despair, rage, and sadness were only some of the emotions that erupted in these spaces as teachers risked professional and personal certainty and moved toward "learning to see differently [that] requires a willingness to live with new fears . . . learning to inhabit a morally ambiguous self" (Boler, 1999, p. 182).

This book is a product of a teacher inquiry community (TIC) funded by the National Writing Project where participants recognized some of their habits of seeing students in particular ways and challenged themselves to see beyond those perceptions—to acknowledge that whatever it is they recognize in any given moment is masking an infinite number of things they could not possibly see in the same moment. The codirectors of the Red Clay Writing Project (JoBeth Allen, Bob Fecho and myself, Stephanie) invited Red Clay teachers to participate in a yearlong TIC that engaged in systemic research in their classrooms focused on one disenfranchised student and their critical attempts to reengage those students in meaningful ways (see Appendix B for some readings on teacher research that were helpful to us). We drew on the powerful potential of case study teacher research (e.g., Cochran-Smith, 2009; Dyson & Genishi, 2005; Goswami et al., 2009) to begin our inquiry. Participants wrote fieldnotes, reflections, prose, and poetry for themselves and then came to a TIC meeting prepared to share one piece of writing about their interactions with the student with the group (see Appendix C for some readings on writing that were helpful to us). We then used an oral inquiry process to respond to the writer and piece of writing in an effort to provide support for the teacher-author to find new meaning and pedagogical possibilities (see Appendix A for a description of oral inquiry processes and our adaptation).

The group's initial goal for the inquiry group was aimed at "critical pedagogy" and the ways in which teachers enacted critical pedagogies to engage the students they perceived as vulnerable. But in the monthly gatherings, our oral inquiry process, and the construction of this text it was clear that there was no one "pedagogical" approach—or even one way of thinking or seeing—that defined the critical nature of the teachers' work. Their work with kids who have negative experiences with schooling illuminates the complexities of critical pedagogy in a way that could be dulled and muted in conversations of whole-group lessons, social action projects, or critical inquiry activities in the classroom.

A CRITICAL PEDAGOGICAL MOMENT IN TEACHER EDUCATION

In busy and complicated lives lived in schools under restrictive and rigid regulations of federal and state mandates, bodies come together in shared moments where some understanding comes to be. The understanding might be small. Tiny, in fact, when we think of the daunting larger sociopolitical climate in which we live. But those tiny understandings that take place between two or more bodies in a moment in time—or across time—hold the very wisdom we may need for transforming *grand theories* and *best practices* in education.

Imagine a chaotic classroom filled with graduate students and me doing my best to provide examples for why deficit thinking about children and families is unethical, indeed, a practice that damages people. But I am faced with blank stares—a sea of faces disconnected from what it is I'm saying, disconnected from *me*. And I make a decision to produce a more personal story that may get their attention even though I haven't thought beyond the telling of the story at all.

"Did I tell you that I was just at a conference for professors of education?"

Some respond with "yeah."

"Well, you wouldn't believe this, but in some of those sessions professors were talking about how horrible teacher education students are. How they are resistant to what they're supposed to be learning. How they aren't quite smart enough to do the critical work we need them to do in the schools," I said.

And then there was silence.

The chaos and disconnection is gone, replaced with a feeling of togetherness—even if that togetherness isn't entirely positive.

We are all here now with no escape.

Two eyes stare me down more than the others and my gaze rests with her. I have no idea what she sees in my expression, and I'm not sure what I see in hers.

"Are you trying to piss us off?" she spews.

Now I know what that expression was.

"Hmmm. I don't think so," I respond. I honestly hadn't thought about pissing them off on purpose; I had just tried to make the abstract concept of deficit perspectives more *felt* by personalizing it a bit. Just trying to point out that playing the blame game, getting mired in deficit discourses and pointing fingers at everyone around us, distracts us from criticizing the *game* we are all implicated in and prevents us from doing the more important work we might do when we are with students and families.

"Well, you did," she finishes.

Our eyes linger on one another.

Some understanding comes to be and I sit quietly with the ambiguity.

The room is suddenly small and we are all aware of our mutual presence.

But it is mostly she and I—the two of us in a crowded, but now intimate, space: the pedagogue who initiated a different way of thinking, and the student who responded in turn.

And the student doesn't like it.

I quickly decide how to make this a "critical" engagement, meaning an interaction that affords dignity for both of us and also allows us to push into an unpredictable space of thinking together about deficit discourses and the role of educators in co-creating more just relations.

"I don't think I meant to piss you off, but maybe it's good I did. Do you think it's true that teacher education students are resistant and perhaps just not smart enough to do the critical work we need teachers to do in schools?"

Then to the whole class: "Talk about that at your tables."

They talked and I walked around collecting bits and pieces of discussion that I hoped to pull together in some compelling way in a few minutes. But I honestly had no idea what it was I wanted or needed to say—I had literally catapulted us all into the unknown by sharing my personal story of attending a conference. Asking the students to talk to one another about the conundrum was not only a pedagogical strategy to get everyone "engaged" or a strategy to buy myself some thinking time—even if both of those were helpful results. I desperately needed to hear what others were saying, how they were using language, how they were moving their bodies and using their facial expressions to make sense of our situation. And I needed to be with them in this meaning-making, leaning over the edge of predictability, not relying on repetitions of the past but working in the unknown to see what would emerge.

It seems a bit cruel in hindsight for me to tell a group of 20 or so preservice and early career teachers that many professors and researchers think they are deficient, not up to the job of properly educating our diverse youth, not intellectual enough to *really* understand what's at stake, and too wrapped up in their own privilege to recognize inequity or be willing to work within solidarity. But that story—that folks were gathering together in spaces and complaining about teacher education students—fundamentally changed the classroom space that evening. It made us all analyze the way we are implicated in the "guilt trips" of our profession—the blame game, a game without an end, a vicious cycle of pointing fingers everywhere except toward the places where the rules of the game are too often formed. It's a distraction from finding our opportunities to be critical of ourselves and in creative solidarity with others. If we are busy pointing fingers at who is to blame for perceived deficits in children, families, teachers, even legislators making decisions about our work, we can't recognize the ways unspoken rules of individualism and competition divide us, conquer us, seduce us into playing by rules where everyone is deficit in some way and no one can win without everyone else losing.

The tension in the classroom didn't end that evening when the last person walked out the door. And though I had been moderately successful in facilitating a discussion about the ways deficit discourses circulate about every level of education actors, the student who stared me down, who accused me of trying to piss everyone off, left angry.

If I had been in a TIC myself that year, she would have been the student at the center of my inquiry. Not because of this event, which ended up being a key provocation that helped us be with one another in new and more productive ways, but because I didn't think she had what it took to be a teacher—or at least the kind of teacher I imagine we need in schools. In other words, she wasn't "making it" in our shared educational context, and though she wasn't socially marginalized by her peers, she was the one I was most concerned about not "learning" or "growing" in the ways I wanted to see.

I made a joke when she walked in the door the following week about being on my best behavior and trying not to piss anyone off that night. She laughed. Then I laughed. But the pissing off and the joking opened up a space where we could meet and try to see one another differently for the remaining 7 weeks or so.

On the last day of class, she extended her hand and said, "It's too bad this class is over; I finally feel like I'm ready for it."

I disagreed with her, told her she and I both did the growing and learning we needed from this class, and sent her off knowing that she had what she needed to be a teacher who would do the same.

ASSEMBLING CONDITIONS FOR A CRITICAL PEDAGOGY

The carefully crafted teacher-research case studies in this book point to some persistent truths in what it means to teach toward openness and solidarity—to cultivate a critical way of being. For example, each of the authors positions herself to *perceive* unfairness, injustice, and openings for change, but the authors don't assume they know what they will find or what kind of change should take place in response. These teachers insist on tending to the cracks, fissures, and injustices in their workplaces that swallow themselves and students whole—they show us how school itself becomes a "giant" to conquer in youths' lives rather than a place of refuge for acquiring the necessary analytical tools and abilities to conquer the giants of life beyond school (e.g., Chapter 7). They may feel relatively powerless in changing neoliberal capitalism in the United States and in a globalized society that stratifies people and unfairly distributes resources (certainly some of the giants facing us all as humans), but teachers teaching for transformation seize opportunities and interrupt the repeating of damaging practices to make something new with youth and families so more people might thrive.

Perceiving unfairness and injustice and acting against it is what I would call a "loud" part of critical teaching. This active critique of structures and practices in society and schools is front and center in most renditions of critical pedagogies or critical literacies. A quieter aspect of critical teaching that is equally important and powerful, however, is working for dignified classrooms and schools where children and families not only can escape the institution without long-term damage but can actually find power and healing in engagement with schools and classrooms. Whereas "critique" is often (certainly not always—a roll of the eyes can be an incisive critique) located in the oral pronouncements of underlying biases and privileges in literature, textbooks, rules, standards, and so on, dignity can be produced in the exchange of a smile and nod, or a hand reaching out, or a touch on the shoulder, or a moment of shared silence (e.g., Chapters 3 and 4). Critique and dignity are not always easy allies in the work of critical teachers, but striving for both and exploring the nuanced complications in achieving both are worthwhile projects.

But I wonder how useful it is to define a critical pedagogy, and I'm not sure a definition or description of critical pedagogies was what we were ever after in this journey. The moment-to-moment use of language, activities, invitations, and exchanges in the teachers' classrooms involved so many different kinds of topics, inquiries, disciplines, and purposes. Trying to assemble those infinitely creative endeavors into some version of a pedagogy that might be enacted by someone else seems not only impossible but also not useful.

Perhaps the more generative path for me to take here is to suggest that across all these very different classroom contexts, there were some shared *conditions* that the teacher had some control over and cultivated, even if at different levels of intensity. But it is equally important to stress that students also had (and always have) control over these conditions, which is why pedagogy must always be seen as a collaborative coming together rather than in the binaries of teaching/learning and teacher/student. In the next section I flesh out some of the conditions that produced the possibility for teachers and students to create critical pedagogies together.

An Openness to Unpredictability

The first thread woven throughout the chapters that assembles our "critical pedagogy" is what I would call a *willingness to lean over the edge of predictability and be open to what might emerge beyond what has been in the past.*

A fundamental question driving our collective journey was how change can be possible in classrooms that are part of larger institutions that have historically privileged some and marginalized others. We believed that narrowing what can be an overwhelming question to *What happens when I focus my attention on a student I perceive to be vulnerable in the school setting?* might offer both practice-oriented and theoretical insights into broader questions regarding the power and potential of education. Indeed, it was in our focus on the more intimate that allowed us to shed the weighty skin of institutional requirements and scripts and open ourselves to being with students and with our writing differently and noticing how that difference emerged.

How does difference emerge? Davies et al. (forthcoming) draw on poststructural theories of self/other to explore a similar question about agency and the possibility of change. They take up an assumption that people are both individual subjects and integrally connected with others—we are both singular and plural. This is crucial in thinking about how change comes to be, for it is not in the sheer will of one individual subject to make change come about—it is both about individual actors and the ways they come into being with others. Specifically Davies and her colleagues draw on a perspective of "emergent being/Being" where the

> autonomous individual is thus not a conceptual pivot for Deleuze. He is interested, rather, in acts of becoming through continuous difference, in which one is not separable from life as defined by others, but *with others*, integral to life itself. He is interested in liberating the body's forces of affirmation, the powers of affecting and being affected, rather than closing down our modes of existence through categorization and repetition. (n.p.)

In other words, if teachers are interested in how change might come to be and how teachers and students both can be positioned as "agents of change," we might look at the generative site of coming together where we are in a mutual emergence of "affecting and being affected." Deleuze and Davies et al., then, encourage us to see potential change, or *difference in being*, as an agentic force through which a different existence becomes possible rather than relying on past modes of existence that include "categorization and repetition."

This volume is a beautiful example of the emergence of *being differently* through the mutual and reciprocal acts of being open to affecting and being affected. It won't take readers long to see that the changes that emerged in these teachers' classrooms, in their actions, and in their students were produced in the moments where student and teacher (and sometimes parents, other students, and other teachers) became willing participants in the unpredictable—a leaning in, if you will, to the subtle initiations and invitations they each enacted and perceived in themselves and others. It was in these spaces of moving beyond the categories and repetitions of school that are always lurking where change came into being.

An important extension to note here is the relationship each teacher took on with her writing and the others who were involved in the writing journey. It was possible, of course, for the teacher-authors to "write up" their yearlong inquiry in a predictable fashion through a mode of communication they were comfortable with from past experiences. But the *willingness to lean over the edge of predictability and be open to what might emerge* extended beyond the teachers' work with students in their classrooms and into their meaning-making with and through writing. Even as teachers sat with their computers and stitched together one word after the other, the meaning they had made about themselves and their students was not settled. They remained open to new ways of being as they played with language and form, allowing difference to continue to emerge.

A Morally Ambiguous Self—or a Commitment to an Ethics

The second thread tugged all the way across this book is the persistence of what Boler calls a "morally ambiguous self" (1999, p. 182), or a *persistent state of uncertainty about what should be done in any given situation in order to be ethical.*

Rather than judging oneself (and others) against some hypothetical moral compass, the teachers here were committed to *being* with their students and living in an ethical way inside that being. This distinction—between moralism and ethics—is useful for educators to think about and consider in their practice. Deleuze (1980), drawing on Spinoza, makes a nuanced argument that morality and ethics are "two absolutely different worlds" (n.p.) where morality is linked to a judgment about an action:

> Morality is the system of judgement. Of double judgement, you judge yourself and you are judged. Those who have the taste for morality are those who have the taste for judgement. Judging always implies an authority superior to Being, it always implies something superior to an ontology . . . therefore values are the fundamental element of the system of judgement. (n.p.)

What readers will not find in this volume is a certain moral stance that leads to judgment, neither the judgment of themselves about whether or not they were "good" or "bad" educators/people nor the judgment of their students and their students' families.

In their search for dignified and empowering pedagogical interactions, the teachers defined themselves against a moralistic stance of what is "right" and "wrong" in a classroom, school, and society, but asked the constantly nagging question "How is that possible?"

Deleuze (1980) contrasts ethics with moralism at the fulcrum of judgment:

> You do not judge. . . . Somebody says or does something, you do not relate it to values. You ask yourself how is that possible? How is this possible in an internal way. . . . How must it be in order to say that? . . . You seek the enveloped modes of existence, and not the transcendent values. (n.p.)

This ethical orientation is grounded in the assumption that we are not only individual beings but also plural, and interconnected with all others around us—human and nonhuman (Barad, 2012). In other words, we do not perceive or act in a vacuum where the right or wrong words or actions or thoughts are available to us at any time. But rather we live through intra-actions with ourselves and others; indeed, Barad tells us, "'Individuals' are infinitely indebted to all others, where indebtedness is about not a debt that follows or results from a transaction, but rather, a debt that is the condition of possibility of giving/receiving" (p. 214). *How is that possible? Or what conditions made this possible? Are then more productive questions than Was that action good or bad, right or wrong?*

The teacher-authors in this book find themselves—as we all do—in particular places at particular times and faced with particular choices. There is rarely anything generalizable about such conditions, at least not in a way that would lead us to then want to tell other educators what the "right" thing to do in any given situation is and what the "wrong" thing to do would be. This stance problematizes a dominant theme in much writing in critical pedagogy (though not necessarily in critical literacies work) where some answers to injustices are spelled out as if they were already known. What we must consider is that the conditions that made our thoughts, words, and actions possible today will be changed as others speak and act. In other words, a problem may not be "solved" but rather new conditions will make new things possible and we cannot anticipate if those will result in something positive that is also sustainable across time and space.

In this way, we see the conditions of critical pedagogy necessarily requiring an ethical stance for questioning and acting and making sense rather than a moralistic stance that knows right and wrong.

A Commitment to the Aesthetic

A third thread woven throughout the chapters in this volume is a *commitment to aesthetics and the assumption that the production of beauty in the classroom and through writing is a gift worth the work.* This thread, like the two previous threads, stands in stark contrast to the neoliberal push for efficiency and the economical when it comes to educating youth. In Vea Vecchi's (2010) passionate and compelling argument for the central role of aesthetics and the atelier in Reggio Emilia schools, she criticizes any culture aimed at speed at the cost of human perceptivity:

> We lose opportunities for *seeing* and *tasting* the things around us. We are not
> helped in this task by a hurried, superficial culture that tends to diminish a
> sense of wonder, our interests and emotions, and *brands* learning with a stamp
> from which aesthetics has been eliminated; the aesthetics of actions, of intel-
> ligent perceptions and of time and rhythm; aesthetics that develop together
> with reasoning and emotion. (p. 31)

Vecchi makes the argument that educators need to bring aesthetics "back to an experience of life and relations . . . and [return] it to the everyday processes which help us to sense *how things dance together with one another*" (Vecchi, 2010, p. 15). In order for any of us to be poised to sense how things dance together with one another, we have to have our bodies' antennae raised and ready to perceive the creative ways people and places and things dance together. And we need time when we aren't rushing around, multitasking in a way that contributes to the emphasis on efficiency in schooling and life.

In the chapters in this volume, the teacher-authors slowed down enough to do two things: (1) raise their perceptive antennae in their classrooms and not rush through and over the fleeting moments that were openings for powerful teaching and learning and (2) spend the time to craft aesthetically provocative pieces of writing that they didn't know they were capable of producing before our project. But we all committed to the pushing into unknown ways of being ourselves, teachers, and writers. We remained committed to the *idea* that the acts of paying attention and writing might hold transformative possibilities.

In fact, the result is nothing short of remarkable. Because we were refining our antennae to ways of writing that were aesthetically provocative, we also began to perceive students' ways of being in the classroom as aesthetic engagements. Jennifer (Chapter 2) lifted philosophical wonderings from a 1st-grader's statement that he was "free as the ocean" to resee this child not as a struggling literacy learner, but as someone with nothing but possibility. Angela and Dawan (Chapter 7) started to see the pithy comments of a presumably disengaged high school student as aesthetically charged rhythms of call-and-response, then they developed a compelling argument that call-and-response is critical pedagogy. Allisa (Chapter 5) found poetry in and through her interactions with a student on the margins, enabling her to see both herself and her student as poetic beings, as poetry itself.

The eruption of aesthetics in our work here cannot be overstated. It became clear time and again that openness to and tending of the beauty of intra-action (e.g., Barad, 2012), the tenderness of small moments, the details of sight and sound and bodies and place, and the wildly different crafting of our experiences in writing *opened up new ways for us to be with one another, with our students, and in the world.*

Try as pedagogues might to bring in students' lives, interests, and critical events in the world to our classrooms as ways to enact "critical pedagogies"—we stand firm in our belief that the creative, iterative work of aesthetics is crucial if we are to have hope for newness in our world.

STRUCTURE OF THE BOOK

Chapters in this book focus on a particular student (Chapters 2, 6, 7), parent (Chapter 4), or the teacher-writer and the change she experienced as a result of interacting with one or more students (Chapters 3, 5). All names used in the book are pseudonyms and chapters are organized to progress by grade level from kindergarten and 1st grade through high school, and each chapter begins with a brief synopsis of the chapter. At the end of each chapter readers will find guiding prompts and questions about the content of the chapter, a particular concept or theory in the chapter, and provocations for the reader thinking about her or his own classroom or about the way the chapter was crafted by the author. Making meaning with text is a generative activity, however, and readers might prefer to develop their own prompts and questions in relation to a chapter. In that case, we applaud your engagement and encourage your creativity. Readers will also find a suggested writing exercise that is connected to the way the chapter was written. Readers, again, may prefer to write from the chapters in ways different from those suggested in the writing exercises. Given our commitment to and faith in the power of writing as a meaning-making exploratory act, we really hope readers will use this text as a way to spark their own writing through either engagement with the exercises or other processes.

As you read these chapters and notice the way the teacher-authors write about the particulars of individual students' and family members' experiences with school and the particulars of their own personal journey of being changed by their coming together with individual students and family members, you might also want to think about the broader context in which we all work. In other words, we want to remind readers that individual experiences are always related to broader social and political contexts (e.g., Jones & Vagle, 2013) and that we should not lose sight of the structural influences on individual lives. The particulars across this book are lived within the context of the conservative South where immigration enforcement laws are among the most punitive in the country; where state citizens have the "right to work" but not the right to organize for collective bargaining and better working conditions; where the criminal justice system effectively controls the lives and futures of far too many African American men through legal discrimination and disenfranchisement; and where educational institutions are largely in line with the national trend of corporate accountability structures for students and teachers. In short, these are often violent contexts—sometimes outright violent in the physical abuse, isolation, and restraint of lives; other times it's the symbolic violence produced through rules and regulations in employment, wages, housing, health care, government assistance, child protective services, transportation, and overall access to a meager and dignified existence that takes a toll on children, youth, families, and teachers.

In fact, the teacher-authors in this book blatantly challenge the ways inequitable and inhumane conditions of society become refracted through the lived realities of themselves and their students and students' families in schools. Even the most protective and critical classroom space, for example, cannot eliminate the high social, emotional, political, and economic costs already paid by students and their families for racism, xenophobia, classism, sexism, and poverty.

But throughout this book we find that hope may just lie in the suspension of the already known unbearable stresses, in the movement of one body toward another, in the vulnerable telling of a story that stitches together a jagged relationship with a school authority (e.g., Chapter 6), or in the courage of looking and seeing things we have been afraid of before (e.g., Chapters 3 and 4). It's not that we believe fleeting moments of suspension will necessarily transform a child's life, but we know they can transform our own, and we must believe that even momentarily experiencing school differently can add a layer of knowing and perceiving that just might come in handy sometime in a way that benefits the child.

This is the critical work we do—critical for ourselves and with others in solidarity and possibility. It is quiet and loud, committed and uncertain, fulfilling and scary, unnerving and healing; and for this particular journey, it all began when some committed and curious folks from the Red Clay Writing Project gathered ourselves into a teacher inquiry community to spend a year tending to and documenting our experiences with a student we perceived as vulnerable in the context of school. We decided to open ourselves to see what we might have been afraid of, to look again at ourselves and others, to relieve ourselves of the pain of separateness (e.g., Boler, 1999) we may not have even realized had captured us into a pattern of seeing and being that might have been too certain. We taught, wrote, thought, read, responded, and rearranged work and personal lives to accommodate this newly emerging ambiguity. And in so doing, we stumbled into new fears, new vulnerabilities, and new uncertainties—all spaces fertile for powerful change. Critical teachers such as these are often isolated from one another, but they spend their days with willing participants for exploring how school can be different in the present and future than what it was just a moment ago.

REFERENCES

Barad, K. (2012). On touching: The inhuman that therefore I am. *differences: A Journal of Feminist Cultural Studies, 23*(3), 206–223.

Boler, M. (1999). *Feeling power: Emotions and education.* New York, NY: Routledge.

Cochran-Smith, M. (2009). "Re-culturing" teacher education: Inquiry, evidence, and action. *Journal of Teacher Education, 60*(5), 458–468.

Davies, B., Claes, L., De Munck, D., De Schauwer, E., Van De Putte, I., & Verstichele, M. (forthcoming). Recognition and difference: A collective biography. *International Journal of Qualitative Studies in Education.*

Deleuze, G. (1980). Spinoza. Retrieved from http://www.webdeleuze.com/php/texte.php?amp=&=&cle=190&groupe=Spinoza&langue=2

Dyson, A. H., & Genishi, C. (2005). *On the case: Approaches to language and literacy research.* New York, NY: Teachers College Press.

Goswami, D., Lewis, C., Rutherford, M., & Waff, D. (2009). *On teacher inquiry: Approaches to language and literacy research.* New York, NY: Teachers College Press.

Jones, S., & Vagle, M. (2013). Living contradictions and working for change: Toward a theory of social class-sensitive pedagogy. *Educational Researcher, 42*(3), 129–141.

Vecchi, V. (2010). *Art and creativity in Reggio Emilia: Exploring the role and potential of ateliers in early childhood education.* New York, NY: Routledge.

CHAPTER 2

"You Just Got to Keep on Tryin'"
Making Waves by Recognizing and Responding to Small Moments

Jennifer McCreight

In this chapter, Jennifer writes about her looping experience in 1st grade after having her students as kindergarteners. Through the use of an ocean metaphor she explores both the riskiness and the safety of a classroom space opening up for a young child to merge his worlds of home and school.

What can we learn from studying one child? Connecting with one family?

—JoBeth Allen, *Creating Welcoming Schools: A Practical Guide to Home-School Partnerships with Diverse Families*

I blow my whistle and begin to walk backward away from the playground, a sign for my students that it is time to go inside. A wave of children immediately rushes forward, playfully shoving their way into line. Mr. W, our classroom paraprofessional, scans the expanse of slides and monkey bars, searching for any lagging children among the darting, laughing kindergarteners still outside. Out of the corner of my eye, I see Mack, who is staring quite intently at Mr. W and me. There is no hint of defiance in his deep brown eyes. Yet there is no movement to join the class, no effort made to lessen the distance between us. He is only 50 yards away, but I see him as I would see a boat on the ocean's horizon; he is still within eyesight, but the gap between us seems difficult to navigate.

FREE AS THE OCEAN . . .

"Why do some children have freedom and others do not?" our class wants to ask their families through our dialogue journals, based on a reading of *The Wall: Growing up Behind the Iron Curtain* (Sis, 2007). Mack, the same 5-year-old African American student from the playground, originally posed this question, and is now quickly and deliberately winding his way to a chair to begin crafting his own letter seconds after being dismissed from the carpet. The other kindergarten children are working around the room to represent their answers in words and pictures. We will later place their writing in book bags to travel home for the weekend, for family members to read and respond to.

My student teacher calls me over to Mack.

"You've got to hear this," she whispers.

Louder, she says, "Mack, tell Ms. McCreight about your journal!"

"What are you working on?" I ask him.

"This is me," he says. "I'm as free as the ocean." He has drawn himself, in his simple way of working with squiggly lines and circles, in the water, and has worked with Molly to write "ocu" (ocean). His long fingers shake, as they often do when writing, in his effort to continue, and he uses the blue crayon to make waves across the page. "Some children can't be free like this," he says thoughtfully, and together we write our weekly question to his parents.

How Free Are We?

Free as the ocean.

This poetic statement embodies all that I, as his teacher, could want for Mack, especially when compared with our experience on the playground. An ocean metaphor implies endless possibility, adventure, discovery, and excitement. There is beauty, the lull of quiet waters right before the crash of another wave, a blue-green expanse that is thrilling in its unpredictability. This statement implies promise—in our case, the promise we will engage in meaningful and dynamic learning as a community.

Yet it only takes one step into deep waters, or the crash of one forceful wave, to realize that the freedom Mack envisions in the ocean is powered by dangerous underlying currents. Time spent in its grasp could reveal either a boy learning to navigate its storms or one swept out into the educational water's vast blackness.

He may have sensed this on the playground, unsure how much to immerse himself in the unfamiliar waters of our shared kindergarten classroom, a protective tide pool in a larger educational ecosystem he had not helped to create.

But by midyear, something in him had changed.

Finding Sandbar Moments

Mack was an intuitive and perceptive reader of his world (Freire & Macedo, 1987), and he regularly evaluated the school space in which his teachers expected him to be an active, engaged learner. Gonzáles, Moll, & Amanti (2005) stated that "the interaction between text and social life, between word and world, is a constant process" (p. 22), and it was for Mack. But it was for me too. Our time together was full of ups and downs, stops and starts. Moments when large tears would splash down Mack's cheeks and in his eyes I read immense disappointment in my not understanding him. And there were other moments when our eyes connected in a shared feeling of camaraderie, and I realized he felt heard and validated.

As a participant in the Red Clay Writing Project Teacher Inquiry Community, I focused for a year on moments of interaction between Mack and me. As I began writing this narrative, my hope was to better understand and explain those times when Mack and I existed together, fluidly moving between the roles of colearner and individual, teacher and student, leader and follower. In conjunction with my writing project colleagues, I stepped back from the hectic nature of daily school life to engage more fully in the tiny, intimate moments that made up the dynamics of my relationship with Mack. It was not easy, but it was a necessary part of our self-discovery and creation of community.

These shared moments of being together immersed in dialogic interactions, when our roles as student and teacher were blurred and we became two people trying to make sense of one another and our work in the world, are what I have come to see as a key part of the "critical" work in the complex teaching and learning I engaged that year.

Beginning to Drown

I had to talk with him, I said, Mack . . . you know . . . you're trying really hard, and . . . I'm very proud of you, of what you're doing. But you're gonna have to . . . get it together, make sure you're getting tight

in school, listen to Ms. McCreight, following directions, and you try your
best to do what she's asking you to do.

—Natalie, Mack's mother

Experience has shown me there is a discrepancy between education's surface-level projection of equality and its murky, mazelike
depths. I have not observed a direct line between the kind of work ethic
Natalie, Mack's mother, expected of her son, and stories of educational
success. Instead, I have come to feel like Vivian Vasquez (2004), who
stated:

> Much of what takes place in schools and in communities where I grew up,
> in North America, is inaccessible to certain marginalized groups, especially
> those who are people of color, because of the way in which curriculum is often
> developed from the top down. (p. xv)

Recalling the experience of Vasquez, my 8 years in the classroom
have shown me that many of my students do not come to school armed
with an abundance of economic or cultural capital—at least not the
kind portrayed positively by media sources and people with political
and financial power (Bourdieu, 2002). No matter how hard they try
to "get it together," their unique backgrounds and perspectives often
position them against the current.

Yet these children *do* come to school bursting with their own cultural backgrounds, ripe for sharing and teaching others. They are not
empty vessels waiting to be filled with knowledge, nor are their brains
full of contaminated contents that must be dumped out, screened, and
filtered before being replenished (Freire, 1972). Rather, they and their
families have important stories to tell, and I must hear them, using
these experiences to strengthen, improve, and even reinvent existing
school curriculum. Mack was one of those students, and his family was
one of those families, and my understanding of the stories he wished
to tell, to weave into his school day, depended upon my willingness to
pay attention to the small moments we shared. Each time Mack mentioned his mother, father, grandmother, grandfather, brother, or sister,
he gave me the opportunity to strengthen the connection between his
school and home lives.

This was not always so clear to me. As a European American
woman educator who migrated from the northern part of the United

States to the South upon graduating from college, I initially welcomed the scripted guides and teacher training provided by my school as I began my first job.

I was young. Scared. A self-proclaimed perfectionist in a profession so nuanced that I now realize the mere concept of perfectionism is laughable. I wanted answers, and my administrators were providing them, all packaged colorfully and backed with research, to boot.

I also wanted someone to pass responsibility to when these programs were not as successful as my school's administration promised. And there were my students' families, standing before me with a cultural background unfamiliar to me, a group of people with whom I expected to find more differences than commonalities.

In unfamiliar waters, then, I found myself adapting to this scripted curriculum and began using families as my scapegoat when students did not meet decontextualized curricular expectations. *They* don't attend meetings, *they* don't return phone calls, *they* don't show up for conferences. I was sending home agendas with daily reports, monthly newsletters, and invitations to participate in the parent teacher organization (PTO) and fund-raisers. I was being a *good teacher*! What else could I *do*?

My self-imposed distance from students' families was a result of this rhetoric, even if I did not realize it at the time. I used it to create binaries, to enforce categories that consisted of *them* and *us, bad* and *good, right* and *wrong*. These categories were unhelpful and had nothing to do with the small, connected moments I shared with students each day.

Taking a Deep Breath

After I attended graduate school, my world opened up. I participated in the Red Clay Writing Project, meeting critically minded colleagues who challenged me to think more deeply about the intersection between my teaching practice, my students' experiences, and my own background. I found my voice as a teacher and could no longer disregard the nagging feeling that the district in which I taught was ignoring the background of many of my students and families. Even more, it was doing so by using the constricting curriculum I initially embraced. I needed to "get it together," to make sure I was "getting tight in school," in order to truly enter into dialogue with my students and their families, even if that meant swimming against the current.

OUR PROTECTED TIDE POOL:
A YEAR SPENT PAYING ATTENTION TO SMALL MOMENTS

"Tt, tt, Timothy the Tiger!" chorused our class, as we sang along to an alphabet song.

"Sssssssammy the sssssssnake!" we continued, contorting our bodies into the shape of each letter and laughing.

In contrast, Mack was quiet, his expression glazed over. He put his head to the carpet, his bottom in the air and his feet planted firmly on the ground, spinning himself in circles.

His eyes shifted toward me. *Was I watching?* he seemed to ask.

He tapped a classmate's shoulder, spinning in another circle for her.

And there were his eyes once again, focused on me, darting away the moment he made contact, as he was spinning again and again while I watched.

Later the same week, Mack and I sat one on one at our classroom kidney table to read picture-driven texts with one or two words on a page.

"A d-d-d," Mack began. His eyes glanced at the picture, then the word he was struggling to read, then back up at me, in rapid succession.

"Let's see," I thought aloud. "Could you use the picture to help you read that word?"

"A dog?" he continued, his eyes wide and uncertain when he answered my question with one of his own.

"It sure looks like a dog! Let's check the beginning sound, just to be sure."

We read, this pattern continuing, the remainder of the book: Mack first attempting the text, me offering a strategy to help him, Mack questioningly responding, and me offering to check his answer with him.

Mack seemed to keep himself at a distance—far away from me, from the other students, and from the activities at the center of our classroom—when he initially stepped into our kindergarten room, and moments where he physically disengaged were common. I might have assumed he didn't care, that he wasn't interested in learning to read, except that his eyes, the same ones that shiftily eyed me as we wiggled and moved as a class, grew wide and concerned when we sat one on one at our classroom kidney table to read picture-driven texts with one or two words on a page. Mack seemed unsure of himself, and even less sure of whether I was there to help him crack the alphabetic code. These contradictory instances weighed heavy on my mind as I attempted to engage him as a learner.

Venturing off the Shoreline

We shared other moments, though, when Mack's confidence would fill up a room. His small stature appeared much larger when he incessantly waved his hands through the air in an attempt for me to call on him during classroom discussions.

"Once," he began, connecting to a book we were reading about families, "my mama, my brother, my sister and me, we were at church . . ."

As he spoke, Mack's body rose from the carpet, turning around and facing the rest of the class. His long-fingered hands punctuated the air as he emphasized each point he was making.

"The Sunday school teacher," he went on, "she said she was gonna tell us about David and Goliath, and I said, my mama told me never to throw stones at *anyone*, no matter what."

His friends sat cross-legged and focused on Mack, their eyes wide in rapt attention.

"'Cause one time, my brother threw a stone, and it *hit* me," he continued dramatically. "Right in the forehead! It *hurt*! And it's like in the book. That's why you gotta listen to your mama."

As audience members fortunate enough to hear Mack's expressive tales, we all learned to listen to each story until its end, not knowing where he was headed, but sure he would get there eventually, and unwilling to silence him in his colorful retellings (Hudley & Mallinson, 2011).

I realized Mack connected to school, to our classroom, in moments like these. When his classmates and teacher gave him the floor, the space to share under his terms, he became animated and engaged in the topics at hand. His rich family history, one where Natasha and his father sat together telling stories, or when the family attended church on Sunday, buoyed him. In contrast, when he did not feel connected to a subject or lesson, he spun in circles, darted his eyes from text to teacher, and became unsure of himself and his ability to contribute. Stories, then, were our bridge, a connecting link to one another, between the unique and varied environments of which we were a part.

Leading Friends into Unfamiliar Waters

When I shared these hunches with my teacher inquiry community colleagues, a close friend suggested I create literacy activities within which Mack could capitalize on his connection to home and family, rather than consider storytelling somehow separate from reading instruction. As Freire and Macedo (1987) suggested, we must "read the world" before we "read the word," and if my moments of connection with Mack were consistently based on his family, then we needed to intentionally connect to this place in which he already felt comfortable and confident.

I gathered Mack together with a group of his classmates who were having shared difficulty in connecting sounds with letters. We labeled a large sheet of yellow butcher paper with "Words in Our World." I told the group we were going to work on being readers and writers, and to do that, we needed to learn some words that were important to us. Excitedly, they responded in turn: "Books!" "Batman!" I wrote their words on the paper, asking them to represent each with a picture, and they busily got to work. Mack, whose human drawings were sticks protruding from circle heads, attempted to draw a "dirt bike," which was a favorite of his. He also chose the word *books*, and painstakingly drew a rectangle in his shaky, uncertain script.

After finishing, they read their words to one another. With the aid of friends' drawings, they could all read their own words and the words of their peers, after sharing only once!

"Let's hang this chart up," I suggested, "so you can share what you learned with your friends, and you can use these words in your reading and writing anytime you want."

Eventually, we used this chart to learn about beginning sounds, syllables, and rhyming words.

Mack's guidance, coupled with my emerging knowledge of the powerful learning that takes place when home lives are honored and built upon in schools, allowed for the possibility of bringing in students' funds of knowledge (Gonzáles, Moll, & Amanti, 2005). His clear desire to share about family and out-of-school activities, as contrasted by his very different responses to more traditional classroom literacy activities, gently nudged me toward a more Freirian approach to instruction. Mack and the others were not interested in sight word drills, nor did they engage with the repetitive writing of predetermined letters. However, when we connected literacy to their home lives, they became excited about the possibilities reading held for them.

If I wanted to truly dialogue with Mack, I would have to listen to what he was telling me about how he learned best. I would need to bring together his home and school lives in meaningful ways, so that he would not "experience conflict" between these two worlds (Ada & Campoy, 2004, p. 32). My teacher inquiry community colleagues supported this notion, suggesting topics for home/school connections such as the writing of *family dialogue journals*, a weekly opportunity to write to/from each student's home. Mack and my writing project friends helped me recognize the importance of connecting on an individual, human level, in these small moments of sharing.

Mack's Influence Smoothes the Surface

Seven children and teachers sat around one table on a Friday afternoon in December, enjoying Lunch Bunch, a time to eat together outside the cafeteria's din. The children, as they often did when excited, were talking all over each other. Mack looked around at his friends, appearing to carefully consider the noise. After hesitating for only a moment, he clearly said to the table at large, "Please don't step on someone's words" (Cowhey, 2006), making the quiet signal for his classmates by crossing his index and middle fingers.

Everyone stopped and looked at Mack, with his serious eyes, coffee-colored skin, and small frame, weighing his words carefully.

For a moment, there was silence.

Then, after a few seconds, Jacob picked up a story he had been telling about the family dog, saying, "Okay, so she ran across the street without her leash!"

The other children faced their friend, eating their food quietly and gasping at the pup's sheer nerve. Their breath sat caught in their throats, forks to lips, until Jacob assured them, "She just ran to a tree to bark at a squirrel, and my dad caught her and brought her back home."

There was a marked difference in the interactions between the children before and after Mack spoke. Afterward, they did not fight for others to hear them; instead, they began to listen. We had a conversation as a group. In this moment, our combination of hearing and sharing allowed us to learn from and with each other. This exchange was built upon our classroom focus on dialogue, coupled with the thoughtful actions of Mack, with his soft, high-pitched voice, and his quiet, convincing demeanor.

As Ada and Campoy (2004) noted, "The fact that students have not been taught to listen to one another or to engage in a respectful group conversation can easily be overlooked" (p. 44), and it took a student's interjection to help us all realize the necessity of this lesson. In a single moment, Mack made clear his reverence for the words of his friends, as well as his deep understanding of the concept of dialogue, which involves listening to others' perspectives without expecting equal time or to change their viewpoint (Freire, 1972). His classmates responded in turn, making a concept that evades the understanding of many adults their own.

In order for others to hear them, they also needed to listen. Heeding the advice of the teacher inquiry community, and their reminders during Saturday conversations that my students needed to share their lives with me, I looked to Mack for how to make his learning, and the learning of his classmates, more relevant. And while I cannot draw a certain line of causality between this intentionality and Mack's engagement, I noticed an element of leadership and risk-taking emerge in his interactions with classmates that was not previously present.

Anchoring Ourselves with Story

While reading together one morning, the students and I fell in love with the one-page narratives and detailed illustrations in *Family Pictures: Cuadros de Familia* (Garza, 1990) and the way the individual stories within detailed small moments in a family's history. Some were poignant, others sad, and others so funny that while I read, children rolled on the floor in laughter.

"Hey." Mack's small voice broke into one bout of giggles. We all stopped to listen to him, the laughter fading. He looked at me. "Can we write a book like this?"

"Hhhmmm . . ." I said aloud. "What do you all think?" When the children nodded, I added, "Well, we could see about writing a book like this to enter that contest I was telling you about." I had recently committed to enroll the children in a student-authored picture book competition only a few months away.

More nods.

The children and I decided to invite our families to a Writing Workshop Night. On this evening, students could come to school to co-construct a personal narrative with members of their family. If they were unable to attend, families could complete the story at home and bring it back to school so we could add them to our book.

The night of the workshop, classroom volunteers and colleagues filtered in around 5:30, our start time, and we set out pimento cheese and peanut butter sandwiches, fruit, and brownies.

Soon after, two families walked in the door.

While the first to arrive helped themselves to a snack, in came Mack's mom with her son, a huge smile on both of their faces as hugs were exchanged all around. We chatted for a minute, sharing stories about Mack's endearing antics as he walked around the room, excited to be back at school in the evening.

"It's gettin' dark out," he said with wonder, as he ambled over to our writing folder box to pull out his previous work to share with Natalie. She attentively listened as he read, very slowly, his words to her. When she realized he had been writing about a time they had worked together on the computer, she exclaimed, "Mack, you remember that? Wow." He smiled proudly, nodding.

This seemed to be their theme that evening. Mack would share something he wanted to add to their story, which turned out to be about a trip to Six Flags, and I would hear his mom say, "You remember that? Wow." The two of them worked together intently, and the encouragement she gave him as a writer was obvious; Mack's mother listened to all his ideas and worked to find the connections he was making. He was in charge of the illustration and dictated what she was to write, which made for a collaborative and effective writing team. They bridged the gap between home and school, and the difficult task of becoming storytellers, of putting pen to paper, became a joyful activity (Nieto, 2002).

I realized more than ever that "of all the many elaborate ways we as educators have devised to 'get parents involved,' we may have overlooked one of the most important: sitting down together and sharing our stories" (Allen, 2007, p. 22). In this one evening I learned more about their family, as well, through the words they wrote and the conversations in which they engaged. In Mack and Natalie's home, learning was enjoyable, and it took place during meaningful interactions around a computer, a special trip to an amusement park, and in the way Mack's mom gently supported and encouraged him in everything he did.

Similar collaboration happened around the room that night, with six families attending. In the following days, word spread regarding the success of the workshop, as children who had been able to come shared their experience with others. Stories from the rest of the class trickled in, written by mothers, fathers, sisters, and brothers. Some were in Spanish, others English, and families wrote all narratives using the two-page spread of our mentor texts as guides. A coteacher, who was a native Honduran and Spanish speaker, translated all the entries from English to Spanish and vice versa, so all authors could read all entries. Just as we had done when reading our mentor texts, we laughed at a story of Daria getting sick on an amusement park ride, felt Julissa's nostalgia in recounting a Mexican Day of the Dead celebration, and cried silently as we read aloud Derrick's heroic family tale of border crossing before he was even born. From these stories, we learned about perseverance, strength, and love (Igoa, 1995).

Together, we found power in telling *our* stories, each as unique as those previously written. We felt camaraderie in completing this project together. We committed ourselves to being a writing community when 100% of our students and families contributed to the text. Mack's anchor steadied us.

Mack was a driving force in this project. His leadership and consistent desire to involve his family in school learning added to our belief that this project was one we would all benefit from as readers and writers. The small moments we shared resulted in significant curricular change.

In dialogic learning communities, a simple "Hey . . . can we write a book like this?" spoken aloud during the reading of an engaging text can become the focus of months of instruction. In addition to my hearing Mack's voice, we more fully became a community in which we welcomed multiple ways of participating.

We all became bearers of important knowledge.

Mack gave himself, his friends, his teachers, and our larger classroom community a break from standardized instruction and from predetermined structures of family participation, because "when you invite parents to become authors and to share their voices with your class, you are opening a door that parents never thought existed" (Ada & Campoy, 2004, p. 67). In his simple request to write a communal book, our door not only opened more widely but also never closed. Our partnership no longer operated under the school's schedule but invited participation that was convenient for all families. Together, we pushed against predetermined boundaries by creating our own understanding of the connection between home experiences and school activities.

Dissonance Breaks the Calm

Still, Mack's and my relationship was not a linear one, marching forward in the name of progress to some hypothetical utopia. Existing in the folds and creases of the successful moments I have highlighted were moments in which I doubted myself and my perceptions.

Once, Mack's mother and I met to discuss his slow progress in decoding words as both a reader and writer. We sat in tiny, kindergarten-sized plastic chairs, talking about Mack's literacy learning.

"He sits and works on his homework at the dining room table," Natalie said, "and doesn't want to get up till it's *done*. He struggles, but he works *hard*."

"I've seen the same thing!" I exclaimed, and asked if I could share a video illustrating this.

She nodded, and we faced the SmartBoard to gaze at a video of Mack working through a writing task.

"Barber," the on-screen Mack began, telling me he wanted to write about this particular vocabulary word from a text about Rosa Parks, whose husband cut hair to make a living (Giovanni, 2005).

We laughed, making our child-sized seats wobble, while watching Mack define a "barber" as someone who "always got to help people get them *bugs* out their hair," his hands waving around his head and his eyes wide to illustrate the point he was making.

And then our laughter faded into silence, as this same boy stretched out sounds in the sentence he decided to write: "Barbers like to help people cut hair."

"He loves to go to the barber!" Natalie said as Mack's face left the screen. "He loves to get his hair cut! I didn't know he'd want to write about it, though."

Mack's mother and I had seen great strides in Mack's learning, but we were also aware that most of the world relied on predetermined standards and the meeting of universalized developmental benchmarks when evaluating progress. When Mack's activities were decontextualized, when he faced more typical assessments of his progress, he was falling short. I had to face the fact that, while his mother and I were valuing his embrace of home and school life and the progress he made within projects like our family stories text, it was likely that the wider education system would not see similar gains in the same light.

In early spring, Mack sat near one of his closest friends, Michael, during carpet time. Michael was directly behind Mack. In tiny increments, inch by inch, Mack scooted back into Michael's space. Each time he did, Mack glanced back at Michael, who was seated between other students and had nowhere to go.

"Mack, can you scoot up, please?" Michael plaintively asked.

Mack sat cross-legged, his hands in his lap and his eyes on me. It appeared as though he did not hear his friend.

"Mack, can you *please* scoot up?" Michael repeated.

This time, I saw the twitch of Mack's eye, but he made no movement forward.

This intentional crowding and ignoring of his friend's pleas continued throughout the week, even when multiple meetings were held between the two of them and Mack promised, with a serious gaze and the nodding of his head, to leave Michael the carpet space he needed. For a few hours, he honored the pledge made by this nod.

Yet Mack continued to crowd out his friend on the carpet.

"Mack, can you please go to Rest Stop?" I eventually asked him, hoping this would give him some time to think. "You can come back whenever you are ready to join your friends."

Mack rose quickly and retreated to the back of the room.

I fully expected him to come back to the carpet, but he did not come.

Instead it was my own feet that closed the distance between us after the class had settled into a writing activity.

There were tears glistening in Mack's eyes, threatening to spill over onto his cheeks, and his lips were trembling.

I folded him into my arms, not used to seeing this side of him, and he collapsed there.

We sat quietly, and eventually I whispered, "Are you sad because of what happened at the carpet?" I felt the tiniest of movements as his head nodded. "Do you know why you were doing that to Michael?" I asked, and this time his head shook left to right, revealing his confusion. "Is there anything you need to talk about?" I ventured, wondering if something else was bothering him. I again felt his head shake back and forth.

After a short period spent in silence, Mack whispered, "Can I apologize to Michael?"

We stood together, both of us wiping away his tears, and Mack walked to his friend to make things right.

What was he trying to tell me, and what else could I have done to remedy the miscommunication occurring between us? Was he feeling frustration that his friend was cracking the reading code more quickly than he was? Did he want me to do more to remedy this problem, just as we had worked together to bring voice to both himself and his family through discussions, family dialogue journals, and coauthored texts? Although we were incorporating aspects of Mack's life into our curriculum, and although he felt successful in his narrations and the giving of ideas, he may have known he struggled more than others in reading. He may have known it was more difficult for him to figure out the complex system of lines and curves that somehow formed words, and ultimately meaning, on a page. His distance may have been a form of protection, a time to step back and test his boundaries and relationships, to see how strong they truly were.

At this point in the year, I did not expect to feel such distance and frustration. I wanted our moments of disconnect to be behind us.

I wondered if I was romanticizing our dialogue and Mack's scholastic growth (Gutiérrez, 2008). His increase in engagement seemed evident, but his performance in more traditional literacy activities, such as sight word recall and individual word segmentation, sat in stark contrast to these observations. I wrote about this in a shared teacher inquiry community blog, asking my colleagues for their perspectives on what Mack might need from a teacher. They read weekly accounts of my time spent with him, and were up to date on his progress thus far. *I'm so glad you already talked with his family,* one community member responded. *Continue to bring his mother's voice, her perspective, into anything you decide to do for him as a reader.* Essentially, we agreed that my next steps in working with Mack were in no way obvious but needed to blend my knowledge of him as a learner with the voices of his mother and extended family. Paying attention to the small moments we had with Mack and with one another could only serve to guide us favorably in our continued attempts to meaningfully connect his home and school lives.

Learning to Navigate Dangerous Currents

It was time for literacy centers, and a buzz of activity and voices surrounded Mack and me as we began to read together. I was going out on a limb, presenting Mack with a text that included more words than he was used to seeing.

"We gonna read this book?" he asked me, flipping through its pages.

"Yep," I replied.

"Look at these words!" he said uncertainly. "I can't read all those words. . . ."

"They're all words you know!"

Seeming to trust me, he used his long, graceful finger to point to each word on the page, slowly working his way through the sentence and checking the picture when arriving at unfamiliar words.

Before he knew it, the sentence was over, and he had successfully, and independently, read it. He looked at me, a bit incredulously, and then quickly regained the confidence that he often exhibited in discussions.

"You know," he told me, taking on the tone of a mentor rather than a student, "my mama told me that if you can't do somethin', you just got to keep on tryin', and keep on tryin', till you get it."

And in that moment, his mama was there, right next to us, encouraging her son with her characteristic bright smile and "That's right, baby!"

"You've got it, Mack," I told him, grinning.

The next words he spoke were, in true Mack fashion, "Is I the best reader in your class?"

Mack and I did not discover a magic formula to help him feel as though he was safe from education's standardized undertow. The expectation that every child's reading-level progress simultaneously was still present, and others excelled in this area while Mack struggled.

But we continued daily to foster spaces for Mack's counter script to exist alongside these expectations, capitalizing on his dialogic strengths while working to overcome the difficulties he had in learning to read (Gutiérrez, 2008). In these moments, his home-based literacy experiences folded themselves into our classroom activities. In our blurring home/school lines, we both grew: Mack as a reader, and me as a dialogic and critical educator.

One day late in the school year, we were doing a noticings activity (Ray, 1999), where students were noticing interesting things about the piles of informational texts on their tables.

No two children were taking this responsibility more seriously than Mack and Michael, who had formed a discussion group and were drinking in the images of Barack Obama and Martin Luther King Jr. peering up at them. I began walking over to listen to their dialogue, but before I had even crossed the room, Mack flagged me down with a wave of his hand.

"Mrs. McCreight, Barack Obama and Martin Luther King are the same—look, in both books they cryin'," he said soberly, pointing to illustrations in each and staring with wide eyes.

"We are researching to find out what we can learn," Michael informed Mack.

"Researching means you gotta type something," Mack responded confidently, and then exclaimed, "Look! There go Barack Obama again!"

With the characteristically serious tone I had come to expect from these two learners when discussing books, Michael said, "I want to change my dreams to see what it was like in the 1960s, so I can see Martin Luther King."

"Yeah, me, too," Mack answered. "I was born and then Barack Obama is already president. But Martin Luther King turned all dreams to good."

Remembering I was seated behind them, Mack suddenly asked if I could copy some of these book pages so he could take them home and share them with his family.

Satisfied with my answer of "Yes, of course!" he turned back around, and was once again lost in the pages of a book.

MAKING WAVES: THE RESULTS OF
LEARNING FROM AND WITH OUR CLASSROOM COMMUNITY

Mack brought his home life to school every day, sharing it with his friends and teachers on a regular basis. And sometimes there was evidence that he brought a little bit of school into his home as well. He did this in an open and dialogic way, developing a plan to involve his family while discussing an important text with a close friend. Mack convinced me of the importance of creating spaces for such learning, making clear that "I needed to embrace the idea of being a learner in my own classroom, surrounded by other teachers (the students, their families . . .) who shared responsibility for teaching and learning" (Cowhey, 2006, p. 61).

These dialogic spaces existed in both our miscommunications and our moments of understanding. They existed in the form of shared journals and spoken words. Through intentional conversation and a desire to co-construct knowledge, Mack and I learned both from and with one another.

In these small moments of connection, Mack showed himself to me as a whole person, rather than simply a student who existed within the school walls. Mack's home life became part of school, and his family became part of our class. We welcomed his mother, father, grandma, grandpa, older brother, and younger sister into our sharing circle, dialogue journals, and morning routines.

Mack and I blurred these lines, which opened up the possibility for me to blur the lines of teacher/student with all the other children. In listening to him, I listened more fully to them all. I brought Mack's ideas for classroom events and family involvement to the forefront of our community, and I saw more clearly the need to nurture and collaboratively create a space where both the physical and mental presence of the children's family members existed (Nieto, 2002).

My dialogue with Red Clay Writing Project Teacher Inquiry Community colleagues provided me with weekly encouragement to continue to push against traditional student/teacher boundaries, and to embrace the small moments within which Mack, his peers, and I connected to and learned from one another. Through Saturday morning discussions and weekly blog postings, we offered our experiential expertise in collaboration, molding the stories and suggestions of others into advice that was applicable for our unique work with students. We were fully present in these times, and our presence resulted in a space simultaneously filled with teachers and learners.

In each case, children and adults worked to both hear and be heard, an unlikely concept in an educational climate that prizes the reproduction and regurgitation of knowledge. Because, after all, "curriculum and pedagogy can either reproduce the inequality with which students are confronted every day, or they can have transformative power for both individuals and institutions" (Nieto, 2002, p. 172). We could conform, or we could transform.

And so we transformed.

In the vastness of the standardized ocean that has become education, my students, their families, my teacher inquiry community colleagues, and I worked through and celebrated a series of moments. We didn't simply survive the waves; instead, we created a protective tide pool where diversity flourished in both our single classroom ecosystems and our teacher inquiry community collaboration. In these safe spaces, we took deep and calming breaths, away from the harmful undertow attempting to convince us of our powerlessness. When we were ready to venture out, we found sandbars to stand on, where we could see ourselves and our humanity most clearly in the form of dialogue and the inclusion of family stories.

Our year was all about these moments, inevitably influenced by the larger ocean, but which blissfully allowed us to defy the standardization surrounding us. These protective pools of growth were big enough for all of our families and friends, who were present in our dialogue even when physically absent.

If Mack has teachers in the future who will support his efforts and recognize both his brilliance and his mother as an invaluable resource in his educational growth, Mack can remain confident and brave in the face of the choppy waters of educational standardization and find his own sandbar. He will clamor out of our protective tide pool to see the larger ocean spread before him and surely be an integral part of changing the current educational tide. But if he is forced into contexts with scripted curricula and standard measurements that don't take into account the academic growth he has demonstrated, I worry that the shifting sands beneath Mack's feet will create extraordinary challenges for him.

And if I can remain confident as an educator, buoyed by the support of the teacher inquiry community and future dialogic groups of which I will be a part, I also hope to participate in the larger dialogue around the standardization of education and the disservice we do students when we attempt to fit them into one-size-fits-all boxes. It is necessary to continue dialogue with other educators around the importance of seeing the depths of our students' lives in the small moments of classroom discussion and activity; for it is within these small moments that we share our wholeness, where we expose our vulnerabilities and wonderings in hopes of better understanding one another. In order for our nation's infinitely diverse children to connect to school in meaningful and lasting ways, this will *have* to happen.

This *has* to happen, or all the delightfully diverse educational tide pools that teachers and students co-create every day will be swallowed up by the crashing waves of an overwhelming ocean of standardization and mandates.

Mack and my colleagues don't want to be part of a system such as this, and neither do I.

Guiding Prompts and Questions

1. Jennifer uses the philosophical language of her 1st-grade student to frame her thinking and writing about teaching, learning, and critical events in the classroom. As a result, she develops an ocean metaphor to make sense of the life of the classroom. How does this ocean metaphor encourage you to think about teaching, learning, and the classroom?

2. A collaborative wiki, monthly Saturday morning meetings, and a writing group supported Jennifer's exploration into her changing teaching practices. How might you and other critically minded colleagues support one another in identifying, analyzing, and putting to use the small moments you pay attention to in your classroom?

3. The critical pedagogy brought to life in this chapter involves curriculum focused on issues of power, freedom, language, and politics—critical topics indeed, but perhaps impossible to achieve what was achieved here without Jennifer's commitment to bringing the lives of children and their families into school in meaningful ways. She specifically uses literacy activities inspired by Freire, one of the "grandfathers" of critical pedagogy. In what ways is this helpful to you? What connections can you make to your own critical work?

Writing Group Exercise

Collect interesting tidbits of language from your classroom and choose a word or phrase to play with. Write that word or phrase at the top of a page and begin free writing to see what is opened up through the development of a metaphor and how your thinking and doing might be changed as a result.

REFERENCES

Ada, A. F., & Campoy, F. A. (2004). *Authors in the classroom: A transformative education process*. Boston, MA: Pearson Education.

Allen, J. (2007). *Creating welcoming schools: A practical guide to home-school partnerships with diverse families*. New York, NY: Teachers College Press.

Bourdieu, P. (2002). The forms of capital. In N. W. Biggart (Ed.), *Readings in economic sociology* (280–291). Malden, MA: Blackwell.

Cowhey, M. (2006). *Black ants and Buddhists: Thinking critically and teaching differently in the primary grades*. Portland, ME: Stenhouse.

Freire, P. (1972). *Pedagogy of the oppressed* (Myra Bergman Ramos, Trans.). New York, NY: Continuum. (Original work published 1968)

Freire, P., & Macedo, D. (1987). *Literacy: Reading the word and the world.* Westport, CT: Bergin & Garvey.

Garza, C. L. (1990). *Family pictures: Cuadros de familia.* San Francisco, CA: Children's Book Press.

Giovanni, N. (2005). *Rosa.* New York, NY: Square Fish.

Gonzáles, N., Moll, L., & Amanti, C. (Eds.). (2005). *Funds of knowledge: Theorizing practices in households, communities, and classrooms.* Mahway, NJ: Lawrence Erlbaum.

Gutiérrez, K. D. (2008). Developing a sociocritical literacy in the third space. *Reading Research Quarterly, 43*(2), 148–164.

Hudley, A. H. C., & Mallinson, C. (2011). *Understanding English language variation in U.S. schools.* New York, NY: Teachers College Press.

Igoa, C. (1995). *The inner world of the immigrant child.* New York, NY: St. Martin's Press.

Nieto, S. (2002). *Language, culture, and teaching: Critical perspectives for a new century.* Mahwah, NJ: Lawrence Erlbaum.

Ray, K. W. (1999). *Wondrous words: Writers and writing in the elementary classroom.* Urbana, IL: National Council of Teachers of English.

Sis, P. (2007). *The wall: Growing up behind the iron curtain.* New York, NY: Farrar, Straus, and Giroux.

Vasquez, V. M. (2004). *Negotiating critical literacies with young children.* Mahwah, NJ: Lawrence Erlbaum.

CHAPTER 3

Allowing Our Wounds to Breathe
Emotions and Critical Pedagogy

Jaye Thiel

In this chapter Jaye Thiel makes sense of the role emotions play in critical pedagogy by using philosophy and narrative to write through her interaction with a child in her 3rd-grade classroom. Jaye has chosen to focus on the need to listen to and share emotional experiences in our classroom rather than the specifics of the student's story itself.

In schools we become civilized by denying attachment. But attachment and difference never disappear just because we declare them invisible. They always seep back in.

—Madeleine Grumet, *Bitter Milk*

My heart was racing.

My palms were sweaty.

I resisted my body's initial response to contort, jut out of my relaxed stance into one where I held my back straight, eyes wide. Instead, I forced myself to keep the curl in my shoulders and my chin in my hand, eyes full of compassion in lieu of concerned disbelief.

None of my teaching practice or my lesson plans had prepared me for this moment. But something in the personal world had, something from my own life, my own experiences. In fact, it had not only prepared me but held an eerie resemblance to the story that was unfolding at the table where this 3rd-grader and I were sitting sharing a moment of mutual respect, of mutual understanding, of shared being. I didn't think she was in physical danger, something that might have prompted me to act differently after our conversation. In contrast, she articulated a truth about life—and living as a child—that made me realize yet again that regardless of our family background, we are never far from emotional danger, never far from wounds that will be carried with us through adulthood.

At this pedagogical moment I found myself vulnerable, open-minded, standing at the edge of new possibilities with this child. It was as if the world slowed down for both of us. Truth be told, I had been so busy, so focused on the business of school the past 2 years, that I had overlooked her weariness, distance, and detachment. This, our 3rd year together, had started the same way previous years had: Brooke walking in the room with big complacent brown eyes elsewhere, not quite empty, but not entirely with me. Inevitably she would lay her head down before the 45-minute block was over, maybe even fall asleep. But her quiet nature, small frame, and an ability to catch on quickly made Brooke easily lost among the more vocal, demanding students.

Until now.

She had shown me her wounds.

It was as if she had ripped off the Band-Aid and said, "See, this is what I have been trying to tell you all along."

I had finally stopped.

I had finally listened.

I ripped off my Band-Aid and said, "I have some wounds, too."

EXPOSING THE INJURY: A PHENOMENOLOGICAL OPENING

In order to understand our own experiences of teaching we must truly stand under them in those places where the bluebirds never fly.

—Madeleine Grumet, *Bitter Milk*

I see the embodiment of emotion in the classroom as a crucial element in critical pedagogy—the willingness to take on small acts of resistance—a way to reanimate our *docile bodies*, reaching across the isolation and divide traditional educational policies and practices have created. This resistance allows us to move away from the notion that students are unfinished and lacking, always seen in the future tense, because within this future tense narrative, education ignores the emotions and the productivity that intensifies in a given moment and fails to notice that lives are experienced in powerful ways in the present tense (Deleuze & Guattari, 1987).

I didn't know it at the time, but it was this particular conversation with Brooke that began my journey towards a more embodied openness in the classroom, a place where I now see myself as making a move towards a phenomenological pedagogy, one that requires a critical approach, a more embodied awareness of teaching, one where teachers are "paying attention to the belongingness of humans to the world" (Dahlberg et al., 2008, p. 46). Of course, at the time I didn't even know what phenomenology was. I wasn't aware that phenomenology involves trying to gain a deeper understanding of experience that bursts forth toward, makes itself shown in, and is illuminated to us in any given moment (Heidegger, 1927/1998; Merleau-Ponty, 1945/2003; Sartre, 1939/2002), or that it involves the times that we find ourselves in disequilibrium with our everyday world, or that we are always in the midst of the tensions of our intentional relationships with the world, catching "glimpses that acknowledge the inherent complexities and conflicts in trying to capture a tentative sense of others' intentional relations" (Vagle, 2010, p. 400).

In previous years with Brooke, I had operated on the assumption that I wasn't going to reach all my students and that there would always be a couple of children who would slip away like notes across the threshold of a doorway. As a teacher, I knew there was a particular performance written for my actions in the classroom. I was expected to "have discrete knowledge of curriculum, instruction and assessment that can be generally applied to practice—as opposed to reflecting *on* and *in* practice *through* contingent pedagogical moments" (Vagle, 2010, p. 394). Quite frankly, I was failing to see what was already there because I was trying to stick to my script of what it meant to be a pedagogically sound teacher.

With Brooke, I had resigned myself to the misguided possibility that she was just "one of those students I wouldn't be able to reach." But in reality, teachers reach all their students, just maybe not in the ways we plan or hope or expect. As Brooke's story unfolded at the table that day, I realized just how much I had missed because of the ways I was negotiating what I was willing to take up, put aside, hold on to, and let go of in the name of "teacher." I had failed to comprehend that "there is no separation (of meaning) between subject and the world; we are always, already in relation to one another" (Vagle, 2010, p.

397), a part of an assemblage unbound by the individual human as the meaning maker, or the center of an organizational principle where we are coming into relationship with the world in a continuous, productive manner, that constantly organizes, disorganizes, and reorganizes through a rhizomatic network of intensities that can not be predicted or territorialized (Deleuze & Guattari, 1987). While Brooke sat there, big brown eyes welling with tears, I was suddenly aware of the embodied threads between us, and the ways in which I had been "reaching her," more than ever before.

THERE'S NO CRYING IN TEACHING: POLITICIZING EMOTIONS

To bring what we know to where we live, has not always been the project of curriculum, for schooling as we have seen, has functioned to repudiate the body, the place where it lives, and the people who care for it.

—Madeleine Grumet, *Bitter Milk*

In the classroom, there always seem to be unspoken rules of behavior for teachers and students, a Foucauldian self-governance (1977/1995), keeping our emotions and our feelings at the entrance of the school building, like an abandoned backpack ditched at the door. It was never easy for me to push students like Brooke to the recesses of my thoughts and teach the rest of the class. Students like her always hung around, flashed through my head from time to time, a residual nagging at my heart. But like a stomach butterfly, I pushed the feeling deep within my gut and allowed myself to get lost in daily agendas and curricular ambitions. As a teacher, I knew I was expected to keep emotions at bay, for they were to be denied as "lower, coarse, vulgar, venal, and servile . . . [serving as] . . . a social function of legitimating social difference" (Bourdieu 1979/1984, p. 7) as well as social control.

So although it felt uncomfortable and foreign at times, I often gave in to the politics of emotion, the unwritten rules that feelings are to be "privatized" and "pathologized" (Boler, 1999), rather than aired out in the classroom space. I believed by getting one more lesson in, one more item checked off the list, I could curb the silence being sung by the students, like Brooke, waiting in the wings. By continually moving and keeping my mind and hands, as well as my students' minds and hands, busy, I had found a way to escape my classroom's complications and all the emotions that filled that space.

When we attempt to remove and detach from emotionality and our bodily reaction to the every day in our classrooms, I believe we create a "pastiche" (Jameson, 1984) where we think we have "equality" and "properness" and "freedom." In our minds the classroom becomes carefully placed routines and guidelines that try and regularize predictable outcomes where we attempt to control the thinking of those in the room; so self-governed that we lose touch with self, body, and emotions and eventually become accepting of alienation (Foucault, 1977/1995). We allow our bodies to become a prison rather than a site of experience and possibility. And when things don't go as planned, when students cry, or yell, or share too deeply, the blame is placed on "otherness"—class, race, gender—resulting in our surprised reactions to the ways in which students behave or respond, labeling them as infantile or immature, problem rather than possibility.

I would like to have believed that I shared the space of the classroom amicably with the students who entered and if you had asked me at the time of our conversation, I would have claimed that I did, even though in retrospect, I would say not always. Instead, I often imposed separate identities on individuals, teachers, and students.

As progressive and critical as I imagined my classroom, in many ways I still attempted to regularize and generate predicable outcomes and narratives to say who people will be (Deleuze & Guattari, 1987). As an educator, I was expected to create "docile bodies," willing to enact " a policy of coercions that act upon the body, a calculated manipulation of its elements, its gestures, its behavior" (Foucault, 1977/1995, p. 138). This docility can be inextricably linked to the ways in which the field of education allows emotions to be expressed and experienced in our classrooms. As Megan Boler (1999) explains:

> Emotions are a primary medium through which we learn to internalize ideologies as commonsense truths. For example, children are increasingly taught not to express their anger, not to question authority, and not to resist those who have power. These rules are taught through differing forms of emotional discipline (shame, humiliation, etc.). (p. 32)

In addition, these rules differ in acceptability for many individuals "depending on their gendered, raced, or social standing" (Boler, 1999,

p. 32) within society and multiple fields of practice, which "allow the most fundamental social differences to be expressed . . . as possibilities for the pursuit of distinction" (Bourdieu 1979/1984).

So when a child like Brooke shares what she is going through and the emotions she finds herself experiencing because of things beyond her control, teachers, who have themselves already become *docile bodies*—tamed—too often automatically respond with a sense of tabooed urgency, closing off conversation.

TESTIMONIAL TRIAGE: MOVING BEYOND THE EMPATHETIC

We have seen the impulses to grasp that which seems to be escaping us expressed in the reactionary back-to-basics drills and in the school reports that encourage us to extend, tighten, and enforce all sorts of requirements.

—Madeleine Grumet, *Bitter Milk*

Teaching is not about escaping or severing ourselves from life's complications or severing emotions in order to maintain social control. Teaching is about finding ourselves in everything that is shown to us in that space.

It is about learning to listen.

Learning to challenge our assumptions.

Learning to see ourselves as emotional beings.

It is about learning to let go of control and power—which are ironically two of the things that most teachers seem to embody really well—and it is about learning to question the normativity we allow, even if that normativity was set into motion years, even decades, before.

As a result of this normativity, I read Brooke the student on a surface level, giving her academic goals to imitate and reproduce, as if she was a fixed entity within an educational centrifuge, rather than seeing her as part of an intricate underlying connective tissue with "multiple entryways" and "dimensions" (Deleuze & Guattari, 1987). However, there is a point where we must realize that as student and teacher, we are part of one another, "an integrated experience to which it is impossible to gauge the contribution of each sense" (Merleau-Ponty, 1945/2003, p. 137). But through this conversation with Brooke, I began to realize that our relationships must be built on something more embodied than performance standards and curriculum goals, both of which are imposed on our lives rather than born out of our experience.

We tend to deny both our own and our students' intentional relationships that take place in any given moment, closing off the mystery of the strangeness, and in turn, creating a distance that is difficult to traverse. We expect students to be honest and giving and attentive. But we often limit this to academic ways of being only. We ask students to play the part of writers, readers, scientists, mathematicians, and historians. But as soon as stories get too personal, too close, we draw a line in the ways students and teachers can live in the classroom, ignoring the things that make us uncomfortable and failing to notice the ways a postintentional pedagogy of embodied emotions could be used in "fostering connections between fields" (Deleuze & Guattari, 1987, p. 12). Elizabeth Dutro (2008) writes:

> The weight of hard life experiences, particularly in the lives of children, is hard to bear. Yet, those stories are part and parcel of classroom life—whether or not those experiences are invited in or acknowledged, met with caring or disinterest, they are always present. (p. 5)

Always present.

Those words cling to me as I think back on my own life and all the ways in which the things I carry upon my back inform my experiences with the world and I can't help but wonder: How is it that we expect students to detach their lives, their emotions, from their learning? How is it that someone like Brooke gets labeled as detached, when in actuality, we are the ones who have been detached—detached from the ways our students experience their lives, detached from taking the time to find out why our students seem elsewhere, detached from how emotional experiences can inform our teaching practices?

It was precisely my need to repair this detachment that led me to deeply and emotionally listen to Brooke that day and ultimately compelled me to choose her as my focus student for an action research project I was working on within our teacher inquiry community with the Red Clay Writing Project. Our community strived to be more responsive to our most vulnerable students and perhaps that meant our project was also about learning to be more responsive to our most vulnerable selves as well. Brooke had made me realize there was still so much for me to learn about *becoming* a teacher—even after 9 years in the making. The teacher inquiry community made me realize how important it was to take the time to explore this vulnerability through careful listening, philosophical readings, critical pedagogy, thoughtful conversations, and reflexive writings both within the group and within my classroom.

Preparing the Wound

When I was young, I spent a lot of time covered in antibiotic ointments and bandages from both major and minor rough and tumble injuries. Several of these injuries were sustained while skating. I loved the freedom I felt when I stood with wheels under my feet. On skates, I was invincible. With my hair blowing back as the wind hit my face, it felt as if I could go anywhere, be anything. The connectedness to my delicately balanced body as I rolled around in circles and jagged lines amid friends and strangers was sublime. Every bump and crevice in the concrete below me made me uneasy, unstable yet at the same time, daring and brave.

Periodically, I would fall.

When a fall resulted in injury, my mother would tend to the scrapes and bruises left behind. If it was a really bad tumble, one that broke the skin, my mom would apply Merthiolate or hydrogen peroxide and tell me to let it breathe before protecting the injury from the outside world, covering it up with Band-Aids and gauze. These wounds were easy to see, easy to heal. And I have found throughout the years that any remaining scars make great conversational pieces when I'm sitting with friends.

Our emotional wounds are not as visible, not as clear. They are harder to heal and even harder to share. Yet "institutions are inherently committed to maintaining silences" (Boler, 1999, pp. 141–142). That is why it was so important that I allowed Brooke to share her story out loud that day and even more important that I shared my own emotional scars with her as well. In this pedagogical moment, I realized that "to be effective witnesses for the testimonies of our students, we need, in turn, to allow them to be our witnesses even when it is hard, even when it feels too risky" (Dutro, 2008, p. 5). This meant that if I wanted to embody critical pedagogy, I had to attend to the emotive apparatuses of experience. In critical pedagogy, our students can't be the only ones expected to share their lives, the only ones who are supposed to listen.

Through weekly writing reflections and monthly teacher inquiry community meetings, I began (and continue) to wonder what would happen if we rediscovered the sacredness of the student-teacher relationship that we have long left behind, forgotten, and put aside to the far corners of our mind? This question remained forefront for me as I reflected on the conversation I had with Brooke. I started to see this as key to building meaningful classroom relationships, but building relationships is difficult. *Re*building relationships seemed almost impossible. How was I to move away from being one that was condemned by the disassociating of power from the body—while at the same time being one who held power over other bodies (Foucault, 1977/1995, p. 138)? I now realize that by accepting and acknowledging Brooke's story and through my own testimony and witness (e.g., Dutro, 2008), I had already started.

Applying the Bandage

The reality is, we can never separate ourselves from that which takes place around us. We can detach our bodies from it in ways that leave us more indifferent and less aware, but the unifying structures, like tiny, delicate threads, still remain, linking us to all that both we and our students experience inside and outside the classroom.

We must share our stories and our emotions, accepting an unpredictable sense of unification, which may be born of an 8-year-old's call—or testimony—that demands a bearing witness and our sharing of wounds. This is not to say teachers should expect to heal or fix students through "passive empathetic" practices (Boler, 1999, p. 166). In doing so, we are pathologizing, patronizing—still ascribing to the belief that emotions are violent and vulgar and inappropriate to publicize. Passive empathy limits us and allows us to remain detached and distant because we don't have to recognize our integral roles in the process of emotional experience and mutual responsibility. Instead, I believe this unification and acknowledgment of emotion requires that we take up what Boler (1999) calls a "testimonial reading," which

> requires a self-reflective participation, and awareness first of myself as reader,
> positioned in a relative position of power by virtue of the safe distance pro-

vided by the mediated text . . . and involves challenging my own assumptions and world views. (p. 166)

I see this as a pedagogical move where we realize our emotions are always in relationship to other experiences, rather than "in a vacuum of outside forces and structures and relations" (Boler, 1999, p. 21). In this sense, we are not looking for a description of the emotion or an interpretation of the emotion that resides in one individual, but instead we are opening up the experience of that emotion in various and complex ways which cannot be traced from point A to point B, in a binary fashion (Vagle, 2011).

It is here that we see teachers as more than just nameplates on desks and signs outside room doors and students as more than just 5-digit numbers or "last name, first name" items on a school roster. By naming our feelings and allowing emotion to embody us in the classroom space, willing to permit emotional testimony and witnessing—even when it makes us uncomfortable—we are able to work toward student dignity as the cornerstone of our relationships.

BEYOND THE SUPERFICIAL SCARS

We come to know another through the world and the world through another.

—Madeleine Grumet, *Bitter Milk*

As busy teachers, we sometimes get caught up in the once upon a time, the happily ever after, and assume the myth that all our Cinderella stories will end with us making it to the ball. We punch pinholes in the lid of jars just to allow the hearts we have collected there to breathe, imparting knowledge no matter what the cost. But "knowledge evolves in human relationship" (Grumet, 1988, p. xix), not in tests and pacing guides and dreams of meritocracy.

The disengaged students we push to the outer corners of our mind will walk away holding on to what we gave as teachers even if that "gift" was distance, detachment, nothingness. They will most likely see themselves as we saw them: as "to do lists" and papers to be crammed into manila folders and filed in metal cabinets. Yes, we certainly reach them all, but not always in habits that are open, mindful, compassionate, and dignified. Intellectual lives matter and are born in the real emotional experiences of families and students and until we can engage all our students intellectually, we will always come up short. In order to work toward becoming critical pedagogues, we have to take on the burden of deciding when to make choices that will hopefully bring about change. This approach is not something that falls into place overnight. It is not easy. Nor is it lockstep and one-dimensional, but rather complex, tricky, and constantly shifting. But I think acknowledging the embodied nature of emotions and their importance in our classroom is a start.

Therefore, the critical pedagogy of emotional resistance in the classroom space should be seen as imposed governance, a way to maintain discipline, control, and obedience (Foucault 1977/1995) as well as the divides between race, gender, and class. Ironically, if I had abided by the "rules" and "nonnegotiables" presented to me as mandates from my central district and building administration, if I had taught within the realm of the bureaucratic definition of "fidelity and rigor," I would have missed the most important opening Brooke had ever given me as her teacher. In the past, I saw Brooke the student.

Now she was more.

I saw past the desk, past her notebooks, past her pencils and labels. I saw the heart of her life—the ghosts, the people, the stories that she carried into my classroom every day, and I began to find a place where I had some understanding of her experience.

As I began to allow myself to see Brooke differently, and as others in my teacher inquiry community helped me see Brooke differently, I could also see myself differently. I began to question my pedagogical choices as well as the ways in which I approached education altogether. I noticed the tiny threads linking student and teacher and the ways in which I had allowed my voice to drown out the voices of students in my classroom, students like Brooke. It was here that I began to understand critical pedagogy differently—to listen differently—as one that involved self-questioning. I looked at Brooke. I saw her eyes and read her expression. I heard her words and I noticed her gestures. I allowed myself to see beyond the routine and the objectives and gradually noticed Brooke as an active participant in the classroom, circulating in intense, emotional, and intellectual ways. This is not to say that Brooke magically fell in love with every academic opportunity opened to her. There were many days that remained a struggle for both of us. But we found ways to connect—a look, a smile, a handshake or hug at the end of the day—which made our relationship a little stronger, a little less wobbly.

As an adult, I see our lives as teachers taking place on a skating rink similar to the one I grew up skating on as a child. Pedagogically, we are standing on the edge, where all is a blur—flying by us in a circular and somewhat lurching motion. Like skating, teaching is an uncertain struggle for balance and speed and flow. As we try to enter the space where our students skate, we are faced with moments where we must make split-second decisions such as when to jump in, when to glide, speed up, and slow down until we eventually become part of the flow, part of the traffic. We learn how to roll, bounce, how to stand on those wheels, even as we wobble, discovering the rhythm of the students already on the rink.

It is here, on the emotive rink, that I believe critical pedagogy begins to thrive and allows us to start transforming our classroom and ourselves. I know that just as in skating, when we are teaching we sometimes fall—scraping knees, elbows, and hearts. But before we cover and wrap the bruises and scrapes maybe we should heed Mom's advice and allow the wounds to breathe, allow ourselves to see and feel and acknowledge the emotions that we so often wrap up and hide from our students, from ourselves, and from the world.

Guiding Prompts and Questions

1. In Jaye's writing, she attempts to get readers to think about emotions through the content of her writing, and she also tries to engage readers emotionally by using certain narrative techniques. Is she successful in engaging you emotionally? If so, where and how in this chapter does she do this?

2. Notice how each section of the chapter starts with a provocative quote from a theorist. How does this influence your reading of the chapter? In what ways does each quote work for the writer and the reader?

3. Jaye never tells her readers what Brooke told her that day. How does she manage to tell a story of teaching and learning without giving details about the interaction between teacher and student?

4. What does Jaye insist are central aspects for critical pedagogy to burst forth in the classroom?

Writing Group Exercise:

Select one or two quotes from this chapter that make you think about your teaching and put each at the top of a page. Then write about experiences you have had as a teacher or as a student that relate in some way to each quote. If you decide to continue, explore using quotations from this chapter (or other chapters) to tell a pedagogical story of your own.

REFERENCES

Boler, M. (1999). *Feeling power: Emotions and education.* New York, NY: Routledge.

Bourdieu, P. (1984). *Distinction: A social critique of the judgement of taste.* (R. Nice, Trans.). Cambridge, MA: Harvard University Press. (Original work published 1979)

Dahlberg, K., Nyström, M., Dahlberg, H., & Drew, N. (2008). *Reflective lifeworld research.* Lund, Sweden: Studentlitteratur.

Deleuze, G., & Guattari, F. (1987). *A thousand plateaus: Capitalism and schizophrenia* (B. Massumi, Trans.). Minneapolis: University of Minnesota Press. (Original work published 1980)

Dutro, E. (2008, March). *Writing wounded: Trauma, testimony, and critical witness in literacy classrooms.* Paper presented at annual meeting of the American Educational Research Association, New York, NY.

Foucault, M. (1995). *Discipline and punish: The birth of the prison.* (A. Sheridan, Trans.). New York, NY: Vintage Books. (Original work published in 1977)

Grumet, M. (1988). *Bitter milk: Women and teaching.* Amherst: University of Massachusetts Press.

Heidegger, M. (1998). *Being and time* (J. Macquarrie & E. Robinson, Trans.) Oxford, England: Blackwell. (Original work published in 1927)

Jameson, F. (1984). Postmodernism, or, the cultural logic of late capitalism. *New Left Review, 146,* 59–92.

Merleau-Ponty, M. (2003). *Phenomenology and perception* (C. Smith, Trans.). London: Routledge Classics. (Original work published in 1945)

Sartre, J.-P. (2002). Intentionality: A fundamental idea of Husserl's phenomenology. In D. Moran & T. Mooney (Eds.), *The phenomenology reader,* 382–384. New York, NY: Routledge. (Original work published in 1939)

Vagle, M. (2010). Reframing Schön's call for a phenomenology of practice: A post-intentional approach. *Reflective Practice: International and Multidisciplinary Perspectives, 11*(3), 393–407.

Vagle, M. (2011, May). *Post-intentional phenomenology and the ego-centric predicament in qualitative research.* Paper presented at the Seventh International Congress of Qualitative Inquiry, Champaign-Urbana, IL.

CHAPTER 4

Las Fronteras

Crossing Borders to Transform Ourselves and Our Teaching

Daphne M. Hall

In this chapter, Daphne Hall, teacher of young English learners, probes the dissonance and transformation brought about by her deepening relationship with a Mexican immigrant family in her school. Daphne reflects on her own inner struggles to achieve personal and professional truth and balance— perhaps a strong foundation for critical pedagogy.

Keep your hand on the plow! Hold on!

—Langston Hughes, *Freedom's Plow*

Luzveya: The woman in the house was hiding us in the back bedroom because I was hurt. When the Immigration came to her door, she told them she wasn't hiding anyone, but they could come inside and look if they wanted to. They must have believed her, because they went away.
Daphne: What was wrong? How did you get hurt?
Luzveya: My leg got hurt. I was hanging by my fingers from the top of the wall. Someone was supposed to catch me when I let go, but he ran off just as I let go because he heard the Immigration coming.

Frontera is Spanish for border, boundary, or frontier. For some, the combination of deep despair and the promise of a better life on the other side of any given national border—but in this case the U.S.–Mexican border—is so strong that they willingly endure the painful realities of the crossing itself. Navigating and understanding the growth, change, and transformation that results from the crossing comes later. In this case study (Dyson & Genishi, 2005), borders are also conceived as the spaces or boundaries between people.

Luzveya, the mother of several of my students, told me what happened during her border crossing from Mexico to Arizona. We conversed in Spanish, as always, even though the dialogue is represented in English here. While this was the end of Luzveya's border crossing from Mexico to Arizona, it was only the first of many other boundary crossings for her, both physical and cultural. As I came to know her, I, too, had boundaries to cross.

As a teacher of elementary-aged English learners in a small city in Georgia, I know there is a story behind each family's arrival in this country, even if the students in my classes have been born in the United States. And I believe that I will be a better teacher if I know more about my students' families, but this is often a difficult prospect. For one thing, a teacher's time for this work is short, no matter how beneficial and rewarding it might be. For another, the opportunities to build home-school communication—family nights, parent teacher organization (PTO) meetings, parent coffees, or breakfasts—are most frequently offered at school, on the teachers' turf, requiring families to do the bulk of the boundary crossing. These gatherings are often large, impersonal, and designed for one-way information transmittal and documentation of "parent involvement" rather than for building relationships. As a teacher, I attend meetings and programs at school to which parents have been invited, but I have also opted to spend time with a single family that has welcomed me from our very first encounters, when my rusty Spanish included only a little more than "please" and "thank you." Allen (2007) offers a number of examples of relationship building with families, and in this story of boundary crossing I incorporate several: sharing family stories, creating a dialogue journal, and considering issues of social justice.

Luzveya's story is a compelling one. I want to share it for the purpose of helping others see at least one individual immigrant as a real multidimensional person who does the best she can with the considerable wit and skills she has to achieve a better life for her children. However, this is not just Luzveya's story. It is also my story and my version of *our* story—how we have each ventured across the various pitfalls of position, culture, and economic difference to get to know one another.

I came to know Gloria Anzaldúa's book *Borderlands/La Frontera: The New Mestiza* (1987) after my initial draft of this chapter. Anzaldúa's writing about her experience of being from and living as part of two cultures explores the overlapping of cultures, races, and economic classes, as well as the particular dangers of being an undocumented woman. In Spanish and English, she writes passionately about the history of documented and undocumented Mexican border crossers and, in many ways, the political and social climate of our 21st century seems not so different from that of the 20th that Anzaldúa explores.

BACKGROUND INFORMATION

Luzveya and I usually have oral conversations, but, as a favor to me, she agreed to engage in a short exchange of written dialogue using a journal that we passed back and forth via "book bag mail." Her youngest son, Eduardo (then 5 years old), was our courier. As a result of my work with Red Clay Writing Project colleagues and of Luzveya's willingness to stretch the boundaries of her comfort zone, I can now share her story and examine what I have learned through my interactions with her over the years. In our dialogue journal, I asked her to write the story of her family's desert crossing and to reflect on her experience of living in the United States of America as an undocumented worker and parent.

Just as we conversed in Spanish, we wrote in Spanish. However, knowing that Luzveya and I have always made many allowances for language differences and difficulty in our communication, I asked for outside assistance in order to make sure that what we both wrote in Spanish would be expressed using standard grammar and conventions. I am confident the Spanish written here is consistent with what we each meant when we wrote it, regardless of the exact words we used.

LUZVEYA'S BORDER CROSSING INTO THE UNITED STATES OF AMERICA

It was the 1st day of school, and 30 or 40 children and adults were seated in our school's media center waiting for classroom assignments. Far from the door, a man sat with four children clustered around him. The youngest, a girl, sat in his lap, seemingly comforted by his presence.

As I approached to be sure someone had taken their names and ages, I had no idea that these children, the children of Luzveya, had walked across an unforgiving desert a scant month or so before.

The three older ones were in my English for speakers of other languages (ESOL) class the 1st year they arrived as 1st-, 2nd-, and 3rd-graders, but it took 5 years before Luzveya told me about the border crossing. For her, the desert boundary between Mexico and the United States was both expensive and physically dangerous. Her story was not the beginning of my education about Mexican immigrants, but it marked a turning point in my desire to understand more. Some of that story follows from our correspondence journal.

[La escritura de Luzveya, Traducido por Daphne, redactada por Gabriela del Villar] Cuando nosotros nos vinimos Omar y yo traíamos a 4 hijos. La niña más grande tenía 9 años y el otro tenía 8, el otro 7 y la niña menor tenía 4 años. Entonces nos aventamos por primera vez caminando 12 horas sin descansar y mi esposo cargaba a mis niños cuando ellos empezaron a llorar porque estaban cansados. Él los cargaba y después llegamos a Arizona adonde íbamos y luego llegó migración y nos regresaron a México. y así estuvimos brincándonos para acá caminando día y noche. El cuento es que migración nos agarró 4 veces hasta que Diós nos dió licencia de pasar. Nosotros como padres nos quedamos sin comer como 4 días—sólo bebimos agua. Para mis 4 niños sólo tenía unas tortillas de harina frías. Eso fue todo lo que mis niños comieron como por una semana.

[Luzveya's writing, translated by Daphne, edited by Gabriela del Villar] When we came, Omar and I were bringing 4 children. The oldest girl was 9 years old, the next boy was 8, the other boy was 7, and the youngest girl was 4. The first time, we walked 12 hours without resting, and my husband carried my children when they began to cry because they were tired. He carried them, and afterwards we arrived in Phoenix, Arizona, where we were going, and the immigration officers arrived and returned us to Mexico. In this manner, we were jumping back and forth, walking day and night. The story is that the immigration officers seized us 4 times until finally God gave us permission to pass. We parents did not eat for 4 days. We only drank water. For the children, I only had some cold flour tortillas. That is all they had to eat for a whole week.

I was speechless, amazed at what she and her family had accomplished. I have sometimes wondered why it took her 5 years to tell me about her family's border crossing and, conversely, why she then told me at a time when undocumented workers were being deported from the United States and from our city in increasing numbers. My guess is that we needed those years to learn about and from each other so that I could be ready and trustworthy enough to hear her story. The gradual change in our relationship and my deeper understanding, coupled with the increased activity of immigration officers in some of our local neighborhoods and businesses, jolted my awareness about the dangers she placed herself in when she gave that account of her journey.

I was honored to be trusted with it.

Luzveya's features animate when she tells a story or expresses a strong opinion. Occasionally, she smiles when I manage to express something funny or ironic in Spanish or when she shakes her head over the antics of her headstrong youngest daughter. Her skin is light brown and her black, traditional ankle-length hair is usually piled neatly on her head or worn in a long, single braid. In contrast, I am a glasses-wearing, middle-aged, white woman with a short, professional haircut, brown hair going to gray. Seeing my own pale skin in a photograph sometimes surprises me when I have spent time surrounded by many shades of brown at school, in Nicaragua, or in Mexico. I was particularly surprised a couple of years ago when Luzveya's son Alexander took a photo of Luzveya and me at a school function. When I first looked at the photo, I was both shocked by my paleness and totally taken aback by Luzveya's strong, tough-looking demeanor.

However, why wouldn't she look tough? In the photo, she is 33 years old, has successfully brought four children across the desert with her from Mexico, and has borne two others since her arrival. Noticing my surprise (Wheatley, 2002) forced me to admit that I, too, have been lulled into behaving as if many of the Latino parents I have encountered are submissive or compliant because they believe that we teachers always know what is best for their children. As teachers, we would do well to remember that immigrant mothers are not fragile or without resources of inner strength. They may choose compliance over controversy so as not to bring undue attention to themselves or their families; they may come to school for parent engagement events because someone has informed them of this expectation and said that their engagement in this manner will help their children do well in school; they may always speak respectfully to teachers and require their children to do the same because they believe that teachers deserve respect simply because they are teachers. However, none of this means that they are weak or without the ability to think and plan, construct and dream. Indeed, as our relationship has unfolded, I have come to believe that Luzveya's actions and responses are very strategic, and I suspect the same is true for most other immigrant parents.

CHRONICLE OF OUR RELATIONSHIP

On my very first visit in Luzveya's home, I accompanied our school's family engagement coordinator so that I could meet a parent Alejandra had already identified as wanting to learn what she needed to know to help her children do well in American schools. As the year went on, I visited only occasionally, as I was still uncertain of my welcome and unaccustomed to "dropping in" on people—even my friends. I usually needed Alejandra's assistance to help explain the school event or piece of administrative paper I was asking Luzveya to sign, but Alejandra continued to insist that I make the visits and that I revive my long-neglected Spanish. She believed that I could communicate in Spanish and, not always so subtly, insisted that I should.

Luzveya always offered refreshments—juice, *pan dulce*, a glass of water—and the little ones were encouraged to give me hugs and baby kisses. At first I turned down all offers of refreshment, not because I thought there was anything wrong with what Luzveya offered, but because the family had very little to share. When the offers of juice, water, bread, or tortillas continued to be made during each visit, I finally realized that I was not being thoughtful in my refusal, but might even be perceived as being rude or condescending.

I wonder what Luzveya thought of me then.

Perhaps she thought I was, indeed, without manners, or perhaps just a slow learner. She may have wondered what our American customs were for visitors, but she didn't give up on me! Learning to accept hospitality was one of my first steps across our personal and cultural boundary and toward my being ready to hear her story.

Little by little, I visited more often on my own, and not just on school business. I was drawn there partly by a sense of obligation, but mostly by a sense of how honored I felt to be invited and welcomed any time I dropped by. I often appeared with books or school supplies for the children. While most of my visits were positive and therefore reinforcing of my decision to continue to cross boundaries to build this relationship, there were also challenging moments. For example, I attended Eduardo's first birthday party and sat with two men who were Luzveya's husband's (Omar's) work *compadres* and who asked uncomfortable questions about my marital status. Were they simply curious that a woman of my obvious age could still be *soltera* (single), or, as the less generous part of me wondered, did they want me to marry one of them and sponsor him to citizenship? However, in spite of awkward situations, these visits helped establish my goodwill and good intentions even though my growing Spanish language ability was still weak.

My ability to understand Spanish did increase, and somewhat faster than I expected. After all, it had been thirty-odd years since I had studied Spanish in middle school, high school, and briefly in college. However, I was willing to take communication risks and to be questioned and corrected when I was unclear. I was also highly invested in understanding Luzveya and others. As I've noticed with many of my students who are second-language learners, my ability to understand the second language I was learning usually outstripped my ability to express myself in that language, but I was still far from proficient.

My lack of proficiency became abundantly clear when I tried to understand the details of the nighttime shooting death of Omar's brother Oscar, the children's favorite uncle. Oscar had spent most of the preceding afternoon playing soccer with them in the postage stamp of their duplex's front yard. He was shot only six or eight buildings away later that night. I had to ask to hear the story over and over, but there was much I simply didn't understand about who was where and when things happened. Further, my assumption that the manner of police investigation in my neighborhood and Luzveya's would be the same really impeded my understanding; when I asked about police involvement in identifying the shooter, I mostly received shrugs, although I was conditioned to expect more concrete answers.

I hardly knew what to say. I could only sit there and shake my head in sadness and bewilderment. Perhaps sitting with the family for a while, being sympathetic, relating my memory of how happy Uncle Oscar had been when we met at the hospital after the birth of Luzveya's last child, and at least trying to understand what was going on was another step that helped me become ready to hear Luzveya's story. That night I also observed for the first time a community custom that, unfortunately, I saw on other occasions: When someone dies and is to be buried in Mexico, people (often children) go door to door to collect money for this purpose. Someone appears at the door with an envelope and not a word needs to be exchanged while a generous donation is given from people who have little to spare.

A year or so later, I fared a little better in my understanding of a stressful situation, though some of this might have been because the children's English proficiency had improved and the initial information was in English. There was a frantic phone message—"Ms. Hall! This is Alexander. Please come as soon as you can! The police are here and they are taking my father to jail!" As before, I visited the family to try to understand the story of what had happened. This time, at least, I understood enough to know how I could help and had well-connected friends to advise me. The next day, I went to the courtroom when Omar was arraigned and spoke to the judge on his behalf. I retrieved Luzveya from work at the judge's request and waited to speak to the judge with a hastily assembled delegation of family members and a translator from their community. When the judge ordered Omar's release, Luzveya and I waited all afternoon at the jail for him. I learned that there is a lot of waiting in the judicial system and that Luzveya tolerates it much better than I do. I am sure my assistance was appreciated and further helped me to become ready to hear the story of how this undocumented family came to the United States.

During these years, Luzveya and I often sat for hours side by side on the sofa to complete applications for food stamps, Toys for Tots, and other assistance. While the government forms were in front of us in both English and Spanish, they often made little sense to either of us. And, just as I admired her ability to wait calmly for justice, I was moved by her tenacity in negotiating our American social services system in order to advocate for the needs of her family.

LEARNING SPANISH FOR BETTER COMMUNICATION

Through all of this and more, Luzveya helped me improve my Spanish. A consummate teacher, she monitored my understanding by my silences, my facial expressions, and by my ill-phrased or inappropriate responses. She almost always rephrased things in easier language before I asked for help or said I didn't understand. She didn't bother to correct all my mispronunciations or bad grammar but seemed to make strategic choices about what to rephrase for me and when to model more conventional usage. When I talked with her husband, she often translated his Spanish into different Spanish so that I would understand what he meant. Now that I am better able to understand his Spanish, she sometimes has to translate my Spanish into different Spanish so that he can understand me.

Does Luzveya understand or speak English? On several occasions, I have asked the children how to say an English word or expression in Spanish and she has supplied the word herself (one example was *applesauce*). It has never crossed my mind to question Luzveya's ability to speak English, to offer to help her learn, or to tell her she should learn. In some crucial way, I think that communicating in Spanish is an underlying tenet of how we conduct our relationship. In general, when I speak Spanish with parents of my students, I do so to help our communication be as clear as possible. I also try to communicate in Spanish so as to reduce the power differential and to reduce the "affective filter" (Krashen, 1981) that makes it difficult for people to learn or to understand each other because of negative emotions such as fear, shame, or embarrassment. Finally, I do so because it is a way to make myself vulnerable, to take a risk, just as non–English speakers are vulnerable in this country. It seems fair to me that both Luzveya and I give up some degree of comfort in order to be companions.

All these encounters with Luzveya and her family—formal and informal, incidental and major—have opened my mind and heart to know her story. Over the years, I acquired enough background knowledge to help me understand her drive to create the better life for her children that she dreamed of when she and her husband decided to walk across the desert into Arizona.

I now think of Luzveya as a friend. I listen carefully to her advice about what to eat when I'm sick and receive regular phone calls from her when I've been out of town so that she knows that I have safely returned. When I asked for her help in telling her story so that other teachers would have a better understanding of and appreciation for families like hers, she assented readily, even though it wasn't a comfortable conversation for me. In fact, I think that the times I have asked for *her* help have been important steps in moving our relationship to something closer to friendship. As one can see in her words below, she wasn't eager to tell the story of the crossing, but she did, anyway.

Mis Jol—Agradezco y estoy muy contenta y le doy gracias a usted y a todos sus compañeros que me dan permiso de entrar en sus actividades Bueno empezando con el primer proyecto y la primera pregunta es muy difícil para mí y mi familia recordar lo pasado pero pues estoy de acuerdo en participar en esto y les voy a contar tantito de lo pasado y de lo presente empezando con el mensaje de las escuelas.

Ms. Hall—I am grateful and very content and I thank you and your friends who have given me permission to enter in your activities. Very well, I will begin with the first project and the first question. It is very difficult for me and my family to remember the past. However, I have agreed to participate in this and I am going to tell you a little of what happened and of the present, beginning with the message for the schools.

IT'S NOT JUST ABOUT LEARNING THE LANGUAGE

> The people often hold great thoughts in their deepest hearts and sometimes only blunderingly express them.
>
> —Langston Hughes, *Freedom's Plow*

Luzveya prepared me to hear her story, but I have also done some work of my own. Not only have I improved my Spanish but I have also become more highly aware of my status and privilege. As a citizen of this country by birth and a member of a respected profession, I was not afraid to approach the judge on Omar's behalf or go to Luzveya's workplace and ask for her release from work for a few hours. I was not scared to present myself at the jail to wait for Omar to be released. I even have a car and a valid driver's license so that I need not fear deportation for as little as a minor traffic stop. In the past I have taken such privileges for granted.

I have also had to admit my ignorance on a number of occasions, such as where the free medical clinic was, whom to approach about free Christmas gifts for the children, or which office to go to in the hospital to get assistance with an emergency room bill. I have had to admit to myself that, because of my position in my town and in my culture, there are many survival skills I lack.

Improving my Spanish and building my cultural awareness has been easy, however, compared to another difficult and ongoing struggle inside of me. Even though I am a generous person by nature and have a difficult time perceiving a need or difficulty without offering to do something to alleviate it, I have found some unexpected greed and fear inside myself. I prefer to think of myself as open and generous, but there were times when I used various ruses to separate myself from the fear of being taken advantage of or to insulate myself from the family's needs. To my horror, I found myself seriously contemplating a relative's belief that anyone and everyone can pull themselves up by their own bootstraps if they will only try—but that assumes an equal and just society, which we don't have. At other times, I entertained the excuse that I could not possibly help all families, so why should I help this one, since that wouldn't really be fair. None of these sat well inside of me. What I have come to grips with is that I simply prefer to share my resources with people or organizations that I know personally and with whom and which I feel particularly aligned. And, while I have given money to the family for various purposes, Luzveya has rarely asked me for financial assistance.

I have especially struggled against feelings of being too emotionally and mentally drained by my work as a teacher to have time or energy for Luzveya and her family. Conducting a phone call in Spanish is still a fairly daunting prospect for me, so I sometimes do not answer my phone when Luzveya calls, and I rarely initiate calls to her. When I examine this behavior, I remember that there are children in my classroom every day who don't have a choice of whether or not to function in a language that is not yet their own, and I feel ashamed. Furthermore, when I think about the calls I have received since I have actually been able to talk with Luzveya over the phone, I realize that almost all of them have been calls to make sure that I am all right or have safely arrived at my destination rather than requests for help.

I felt less isolated as a teacher when I read about the work and frustrations of refugee resettlement workers in Clarkston, Georgia, comforted to know about other individuals who were making genuine efforts to be both friend and advocate to immigrants. In *Outcasts United* (St. John, 2009), stories about others who work with immigrants illuminate feelings of being overwhelmed by the enormity of their struggle at times. The work was referred to as having a "Sisyphean quality" that led to frustrations and "the steady accrual of disappointment [and] eventually led to burnout." Those who remained committed to the difficult work of attempting to connect refugees to the resources they needed "tended not to strike a balance between their private lives and the lives of the refugees" or were capable of reframing their work to perceive the benefits as greatly outweighing the challenges (p. 220).

Such a reframing described by St. John (2009) has become true for me. As I've spent time with Luzveya and her family, the benefits visibly and easily outweigh the frustrations. The pleasure of watching her children grow, mature, and succeed has provided a good balance to my perception of the practically overwhelming obstacles that the family faces. In that vein, I want to reflect on some of the internal and professional rewards of getting to know more about the ongoing story of Luzveya and her family.

HOW HAVE I BEEN TRANSFORMED?

First and foremost, in a professional sense, Luzveya has helped me debunk or deconstruct any stereotypical image I might have had of compliant Latina mothers who unquestioningly agree with whatever decisions we educators make about their children's schooling (to retain them or place them in special education, for example). This stereotype has been tricky for me to untangle, because I have not been very successful in getting parents to tell me what they are thinking during these decision making meetings. For example, teachers advocated for Luzveya's eldest daughter, Margarita, to be in a special education program primarily for academic reasons, but Luzveya might have judged that this different program could provide other advantages and support. Perhaps she attended the meeting and made some judgments about the character of the teacher who would be working with Margarita and based her decision on that conclusion. As it turned out, this teacher became a strong advocate for Margarita and for the family, so it is possible that Luzveya's astute observation and evaluation was effective in terms of her goals for her family. I saw this play out with other educators Luzveya reached out to in the middle school her other children attended, as well.

So, for whatever reasons, Luzveya has consistently refused to critique the teachers of her children, even when I invited and encouraged to do so. In fact there were many times when I witnessed disrespectful treatment of Latino children and really wanted to put words in her mouth! The question in the following portion of our correspondence was one of my many attempts to encourage her to suggest additional or more appropriate actions that teachers might take or strategies they might use to provide better service to her children and those of other immigrant families.

[Ms. Hall escribe] Si pudiera mandar un mensaje a los maestros . . . ¿qué quisiera decir? ¿Qué necesitamos saber para entenderles bien a usted y a su familia?

[Luzveya responde] Esto es para todos los maestros pues yo quisiera darles las gracias a todos los maestros que son tan buenos y amables con los niños inmigrantes especialmente con los niños hispanos porque es una tristeza contarles que nosotros como padres nos ponemos a morir con nuestros hijos para darles una vida mejor y les agradecemos tanto que no podemos pagarles nunca lo que hacen por nuestros hijos porque ustedes como maestros son como sus segundos padres porque el inglés es una muy buena ayuda para su futuro de los niños inmigrantes porque ellos saben los dos idiomas y pueden conseguir trabajo muy fácil no como nosotros que nos tratan como esclavos y nos pagan una miseria y todavía nos maltratan siempre por no hablar inglés

Bueno me despido agradeciéndoles todo lo que hacen por nuestros hijos. Gracias a todos los maestros

Atentamente su servidora y que siempre les estará dando las Gracias Luzveya S.

[Ms. Hall writes] If you could send a message to teachers . . . what would you say? What do we all need to know in order to understand your family well?

[Luzveya responds] This is for all of the teachers. Well, I want to give thanks to all of the teachers that are so good and nice to the immigrant children—especially with the Hispanic children, because, tragically, we parents have put ourselves in a position to die with our children in order to give them a better life. We are so grateful yet we cannot pay anything for that which they do with our children. You as teachers are like second parents because English is a very good help for the future of immigrant children. Because they know two languages, they can easily get work, unlike ourselves who are treated like slaves and paid a pittance and always mistreated simply because we don't speak English.

Very well, I will close with appreciation for all that the teachers do with our children. Thank you to all of the teachers.

Cordially, your servant who will always be giving you thanks, Luzveya S.

In the response above, Luzveya responds with gratitude to the teachers who are like second parents. On the other hand, perhaps a reminder that we have the responsibilities of second parents is all educators should need.

Taking a longer and broader view of Luzveya's life in this country, she seems deliberate and strategic in her actions and advocacy on behalf of her children, including the cultivation of a relationship with me, one of her children's teachers. If she has agreed with decisions the school has made on their behalf in order to be perceived as caring and competent or for any other reason, then she has done so with a specific goal in mind. She sees the learning of English as the key to success, and she shows appreciation for those who help her children learn it. She has maintained a constant focus on the reason she was willing to die with her family in the desert—the opportunity for a better life.

Maestra—
estoy muy agradecida con usted y con todos sus compañeros que me ayudan a compartir los recuerdos de sufrimiento, dolor y el peligro de morir en la frontera mientras tratábamos de cruzar para tener una vida mejor y las lágrimas que derramamos al dejar a nuestros padres, los míos y los de mi esposo en México. . . .
Pero también estoy muy orgullosa porque ustedes son como nuestra familia, cuando necesiten venir a visitarnos aquí está su pobre trailer, aunque sin techo, uno no deja a los amigos.
—Luzveya

Teacher—
I am very grateful to you and your friends that you are helping me share memories of the suffering, pain, and danger of dying on the

border while trying to cross for a better life and for the tears we shed over leaving our parents, mine and my husband's, in Mexico. . . .

I am also proud because you all are like our family. When you need to come to visit us, here is your poor old trailer, but, even without a roof, one does not leave one's friends.
—Luzveya

If I had any doubt about Luzveya's ability to critique the actions of others, her responses to my questions and comments about some of the business owners and workers she has encountered contrasted markedly with the ones she made about the teachers of her children. The following passage was written not long after Luzveya lost her job in a local plant.

[Ms. Hall escribe] Si pudiera mandar un mensaje . . . a los dueños de las fábricas, ¿qué quisiera decir?
[Luzveya responde] Después de que llegamos aquí fue muy difícil también porque vivíamos como 15 personas en un apartamento y fue duro alimentar y vestir a mis niños. Bueno y quisiera mandarles un mensaje también a los dueños de las fábricas y de los trabajos que si ellos supieran todo lo que se sufre para pasar la frontera no nos tratarían como ellos nos tratan porque cuando una persona hispana entra a un trabajo lo señalan como si uno no valiera nada y nos tratan muy mal siendo que uno trabaja tan bien como cualquier otra persona. Bueno yo me despido sabiendo que aguanté las peores amenaza. El chiste es que nos dan trabajo aún cuando el sueldo es poco pero esas personas no se ponen a pensar que nosotros estamos sufriendo para darles un buen futuro a nuestros hijos. Gracias por todo y me despido
—Luzveya.

[Ms. Hall writes] If you could send a message to . . . the factory owners, what would you say?
[Luzveya responds] It was still difficult after we arrived here, because we were living with about 15 people in one apartment, and it was a hardship to feed and clothe my children. Very well, and I would like to send a message also to the factory owners and the workers. If they only knew how much we suffered in order to cross the border, they would not treat us the way they do. When a Hispanic person begins a job, they designate us as worthless and treat us badly, even though we

work as well as any other person. Very well, I will leave them, knowing that I withstood the worst threats. The joke is that they give us the work even though the salary is very small. But these people do not stop to think about what we are suffering in order to give a good future to our children. Thank you for everything, and I will close.
—Luzveya

Luzveya serves as a model of an indomitable spirit to me. How does she persevere in spite of a seemingly unending array of obstacles? Is it by her faith? When she wrote about finally achieving the desert crossing, she stated, "God gave us permission to pass." A common expression she uses about things that may or may not happen (regarding a job application or a court appearance, for example) is "Vamos a ver que Diós dice" (We will see what God says).

Less than a year before I wrote this chapter, a legally documented immigrant worker at the plant where she had worked for 5 years was caught stealing and was fired. The woman was angry. She told the plant manager that she had a list of 20 workers who were illegally documented and that, if the manager didn't fire them all, she would turn the list over to Immigration who would come in and shut the plant down for hiring illegal workers. This was a brutal blow to Luzveya and the other workers who were fired.

I was out of town when this happened but received a phone message from a distraught Luzveya. Even with support from other Spanish speakers, I could barely understand it. Yet only a few days later, she had reconciled her anger and fear about her family's ability to survive and was ready to move on. When I returned to town and was able to talk with her in person, she did not waste time or energy on the person who caused her and a number of others to lose their jobs. "For all that she did to us, she will not be happy or find work. God will punish her." Sure enough, a few weeks later, Luzveya pointedly reported to me that someone had talked to the woman's husband and, indeed, no one would hire her. Luzveya was not smug in this reporting, as I might have been. According to her, she had left it in God's hands, and that was that.

When we finally discussed the firings at the plant, Luzveya had already talked with an acquaintance who thought she could get her a job at a fast food restaurant. While she claimed to have taken a rest after being let go, I knew that she had continued to support her family by making and selling bread, *atole*, and tamales. Soon, she acquired a job cleaning houses and offices. I suspect that Luzveya's consistent ability to rise above difficult circumstances comes from two deeply held beliefs—that everything that happens in life is not within one's control and that one must do whatever it takes to provide for one's family.

IMPLICATIONS: TRANSFORMING OURSELVES

So, truly, what is the relationship that Luzveya and I share? Am I deceiving myself by thinking that we are friends? With time and reflection, I see that she has been deliberate in her actions and her advocacy, as have I. In this way, I suspect that we have each cultivated our friendship for our own purposes. Perhaps, along the way, Luzveya might have thought, "Here is a person who cares about my children and their future. How can I keep her in our lives, in our circle of support?" And, while it was long ago, I am certain that my thinking might have had a similar element: "Here is a person who welcomes me to her home, is kind to me, and is willing to share her family with me and help me improve my ability to communicate in Spanish. What can I do to maintain this relationship?" In her habit of initiating contact often and consistently welcoming me to her home, Luzveya sometimes seems a better friend to me than I am to her.

In contrast, I have kept her apart from my daily life. I have not invited her to my home, and I have rarely been the person who initiated contact. I wonder if my strong sense of myself as the teacher of her children and of her as their mother has encouraged this response in me. Admittedly, she constantly calls me "Maestra" (teacher) in casual conversation, so she plays a part in maintaining some version of a hierarchical relationship as well. I sometimes wonder if I have tried to create or maintain some sort of control in my relationship with her by way of my status of teacher in a way that is disrespectful. I really don't think so.

Because of the boundaries of language, class, culture, and status that we continue to span as we reach out to each other, I believe her constant reference to me as "Maestra" is a key for the ways our relationship is properly defined. She doesn't need me as a friend who might give an opinion about how to cook chicken or potty-train a child and I don't need her as a friend to advise me about what professional workshops to choose or which trails to hike. We need each other so that her children (my students) and others like them will have a better chance for success here in the United States. The fact that we have emerged as friends in addition to the usual parent-teacher relationship is a testament to the ability and willingness we each have to step outside our usual comfort zones.

We have learned to trust each other.

It is important to tell this story now because times are harder. La Migra (Immigration) is often in their neighborhood knocking on doors; immigration status is verified for anyone put in jail, even for misdemeanors; the children are older and getting closer to adulthood; the oldest son is now in high school and taking honors classes. What will happen when he applies to college but is not a documented citizen? How many obstacles and disappointments are left to endure? How many other intelligent, hardworking young people will lose the opportunity to make critical contributions to our community?

Just as the resettlement workers in Clarkston felt that others outside their community needed to know and care about their difficulties, I believe these are problems that more people need to know and care about. Perhaps by hearing Luzveya's story, more people *will* care about them.

CONCLUSION

Keep your hand on the plow! Hold on!

—Langston Hughes, *Freedom's Plow*

Now what? I promised Luzveya that I would share her story to help others understand. How will I do that? What part will this writing play? What other ways might I find to share what I've learned as Luzveya and I have negotiated boundaries to transform ourselves? How does this relate to what I have discovered about critical pedagogy?

For me as a teacher, critical pedagogy resides in relationship: relationship as it exists in small personal moments rather than grand public displays; relationship as it gives access to and honors the skills, knowledge, and values of students and families; and relationship as it provides the impetus to work hard to learn a shared language. In my case, this language learning meant to learn another language, literally. For some, it might be the language of adolescents or of digital natives. It is clear to me that nothing moves forward without shared language.

Luzveya and I began and continued our boundary-crossing relationship by recognizing and being open to even the smallest of gestures as we reached out to each other. It was important for her to serve me refreshments in her home just as it was important for me to accept it. It was important to both of us to celebrate her children's transitions from one level of schooling to another. As we got to know each other, the gestures became natural and more elaborated in form.

As our relationship enlarged to include more knowledge about each other's lives, I became privy to details of family life, details that, over time, revealed Luzveya's high expectations for her children's performance and competence at home. During one visit, I was surprised to hear Luzveya casually direct her 11-year-old son to bathe the baby, and equally surprised that he did so without complaint. On another visit, I heard the pride in her voice when she said that 10-year-old Esther could now prepare the *masa* as well as form it and cook it into tortillas. On yet another visit, I rounded the trailer to encounter the family engaged in a full-scale chicken-butchering operation, and on another I observed Luzveya's teenage sons on the roof of the trailer competently making repairs. In terms of my pedagogy, honoring, welcoming, and using students' funds of knowledge (Moll et al., 1992) as a springboard for learning academic skills is only logical—but also impossible if I don't have a relationship, over time, that makes me privy to this information.

Knowing the competencies of children like Luzveya's in their homes helps me consider writing pedagogy in an entirely different manner. Why should I ask a child to write about how to make a jelly sandwich when he or she already knows how to turn a live chicken into soup? If I know information about their funds of knowledge, I can help students focus on their topic discovery and development rather than on a topic of my choosing that I have tried to make simple enough for everyone in the class to access. Not only have I engaged them in a more inquiry-driven activity, I have also given a strong message that who they are at home is valuable and honored asset in the classroom.

Finally, my critical pedagogy required me to learn the language. More important, it required me to learn the language *from Luzveya*. I think that "learning the language" is both a literal and figurative construct. In a literal sense, our relationship would not have moved forward without a common language. Figuratively, "learning the language" means to take risks, to open myself to the fear of not knowing the outcome. Placing myself in the role of learner was probably the ultimate equalizer when there were such disparities in status and power. Asking Luzveya to teach me both honored her and gave her equal responsibility in our relationship.

At the beginning of this chapter, I posed the question of how Luzveya and I might know whether the risks of crossing physical, cultural, and interpersonal boundaries were worth it. I don't think that we can fully know the answer yet. I have learned enough to become a better teacher and world citizen, and that is a strong start. Luzveya and her husband were willing to risk their lives to cross the Mexican-U.S. border because America promised a better life for their family. Their oldest children now have permits that will allow them to work here legally and their youngest children, born here, are United States citizens.

I believe that Luzveya *will* experience that better life.

The segments of "Freedom's Plow" by Langston Hughes used throughout this chapter represent the journey that Luzveya and I have taken together, and now we are holding on as the plowing of freedom continues. And in the spirit of always trying to understand, I offer my halting, stumbling, faulty, and incomplete thoughts about how I have been trying to cross the *fronteras* of culture, status, and identity for the benefit of our students, ourselves, and our world.

I would not know the importance Luzveya places on her children's abilities to be responsible and effective at home and beyond. How many boys and girls can both pluck feathers from a scalded chicken and make the honor roll? Fix a bicycle and create award-winning art? Repair the roof and translate conversations with businesses and community agencies? Make tortillas from scratch and excel in all school subjects? Bathe a baby and search the Internet for a new family vehicle? I wonder what else I might learn about the funds of knowledge (Moll et al., 1992) of this and other immigrant families.

For my part, I have opened myself to feelings of discomfort, fear, and the possibility of failure. More important, I haven't stopped there. I have worked to analyze and embrace those feelings and have moved beyond them *poco a poquito*—knowing, of course, that I will always make mistakes and that there will be more disquieting boundaries to cross. I have become a more open, less fearful person.

I needn't cross a desert to keep learning.

I can simply walk across a crowded cafeteria to sit with a family, smile, and reach out my arms to hold the baby while the mother eats her dinner at school family night. Offering to hold the baby requires no verbal language at all, and yet a shared understanding. I don't have to know all families well. And I am now more certain that there is great value in building a deep relationship with one person, in crossing many boundaries together.

This is my final thought about critical pedagogy: Occasionally, if we have enough opportunity and privilege, we can open our own doors (pull ourselves up by our own bootstraps, as it were). More often, however, we need help unlocking doors and taking the first steps through them. For myself, I hope to both offer and ask for help with the doors and barriers more often.

Just as I have remarked on the importance of small moments over grand events, I think that the next steps for Luzveya and me will not involve sweeping changes in our relationship but will consist of small gestures and conversations that gradually take on deeper and more difficult subjects. We have managed to negotiate many of the dangers and pitfalls of a relationship across differences: patronizing or submissive behavior, misunderstanding of meaning or language, and fear or resentment of differences. We have earned mutual trust so that future problems stand a chance of being solved before they cause the end of our relationship. Because of Luzveya, I know that the struggle, the discomfort, the learning, and the tilling of the ground with freedom's plow will help us live lives larger than we ever imagined.

Guiding Prompts

1. Notice Daphne's use of Langston Hughes's "Freedom's Plow" in this chapter. How, specifically, is she using the poem and in what ways does this influence your reading of the chapter?
2. Think about a time when you crossed a border in relationship with someone. In what way were you changed by that encounter? What are the implications of this encounter and the change you experienced in terms of your work?
3. Consider the differences between small personal gestures and large public ones. In what ways have others reached out to you in small and large ways and how have you responded? What small gestures have you used to build relationships that cross *fronteras* with students and families?
4. How might "Freedom's Plow" be used as a metaphor for critical pedagogy?

Writing Group Exercise

Daphne used lines from the poem "Freedom's Plow" as section headers because they resonated with her experience and provided an opportunity to cast Luzveya's story into the larger arena of struggle for dignity and respect. After you write a story about your own teaching/learning or a student or family, search for poems that might work as organizational structures that will also deepen or expand the reader's interpretation of the story you are writing. Then you might play with lines from a poem to strengthen and deepen your thinking and writing. Remember to bring the reader, writer, poem, and story together somewhere in the writing, as Daphne has done here at the end of her chapter.

REFERENCES

Allen, J. (2007). *Creating welcoming schools: A practical guide to home–school partnerships with diverse families.* New York, NY: Teachers College Press.

Anzaldúa, G. (1987). *Borderlands/La frontera: The new mestiza.* San Francisco, CA: Aunt Lute Books.

Dyson, A. H., & Genishi, C. (2005). *On the case: Approaches to language and literacy research.* New York, NY: Teachers College Press.

Hughes, L. (1943, April). Freedom's plow. *Opportunity: Journal of Negro Life, 21,* 66–69.

Krashen, S. (1981). *Second language acquisition and second language learning.* Englewood Cliffs, NJ: Prentice-Hall.

Moll, L., Amanti, C., Neff, D., & Gonzáles, N. (1992). Funds of knowledge for teaching: Using a qualitative approach to connect homes and classrooms. *Theory into Practice, 31*(2), 132–141.

St. John, W. (2009). *Outcasts united: A refugee team, an American town.* New York, NY: Spiegel & Grau.

Wheatley, M. J. (2002). *Turning to one another: Simple conversations to restore hope to the future.* San Francisco, CA: Berrett-Koehler.

CHAPTER 5

Powerful Poetic Inquiry
A Practitioner's Turn to Craft, Revision, and Critical Teaching

Allisa Hall

In this chapter Allisa, a middle school language arts teacher, describes her developing process of poetic inquiry into her work as a teacher. Allisa uses poetry writing and revision as a tool to help her enact a critical stance in her classroom practice.

The poems [in the beginning] are like a table on which one places interesting things one has found on one's walks: a pebble, a rusty nail, a strangely shaped root, the corner of a torn photograph, etc. . . . where after months of looking at them and thinking about them daily, certain surprising relationships, which hint at meaning, begin to appear.

—Charles Simic

AN INTRODUCTION TO A STUDENT AND FRAGMENTS ON A POET'S TABLE

Ray didn't just walk into my classroom. His stride had purpose and a fierce determination to make me sit up and take notice, and I did just that when he plopped into a seat up front. I remember now how he leaned back in a seemingly casual slouch, but I would never characterize his personality as easygoing.

Hungry was more like it.

In my face.

Yes, Ray was searching for something when he presented himself in my life.

I still don't understand why he chose to engage me the way he did. After all, to look at us from the outside, we are clearly different people. He is what some might call a "streetwise," African American young person with an attitude that can best be described as fierce bravado. I am a reserved, even shy, European American woman teacher. He is a teenager. I am middle aged.

Yet his purposeful posture was an invitation, something like an unspoken *Game On* choosing of me. The ball was in my court. Would I choose him back? Ruth Behar (2008) wrote, "The most charged intellectual insights occur precisely when one's ethnographic work and one's life crash into each other in a head-on collision" (p. 63). Ray had certainly captured my attention as I was cultivating my ethnographic eyes, ears, and sensibilities. He constantly acted out in my language arts classroom and didn't seem bothered by the consequences (silent lunch and detention) I administered for his actions—at first protecting my position as teacher-authority in the classroom. I remember thinking at the time what we had discussed in our Red Clay Teacher Inquiry Community: If I could only make sense of what was going on with Ray, I'd somehow be a better teacher. I wasn't expecting a head-on collision, but that is precisely what I got—and the tiny details from my classroom began accumulating on my table from which poetry would grow.

Toi Derricotte (1997), in her poetic memoir, *The Black Notebooks: An Interior Journey*, wrote, "Every identity breaks down to some self that has to learn to live between loneliness and connection" (p. 78). This identity breakdown was a large part of the uneasy tension I found through writing poetry. Ray's classroom dialogue journal portrayed a young man in conflict. He was fiercely protective, yet critical of and disappointed in his mother. He was angry with her for the choices she made, and he wrote about feeling ignored at home. He acted out and misbehaved in class, but I could use his writing to imagine his actions as tactics for getting noticed. Ray even seemed pleased when our team called a parent-teacher conference to discuss his behavior. For 30 minutes his mother's attention was focused on him, and even as she shared her exasperation and disappointment with him in front of teachers from the school, Ray seemed glad that she was there.

Ray used his journal to vent some of the hostility he felt, and he used the journal to connect to me as well. There was a push and pull of trust and mistrust reflected in his writing and in his interactions with me. For instance, he carried his notebooks with him at all times, whereas the other young people left their journals in my classroom. He did, however, write in them without fail, so I pretended not to notice him carrying them away. He seemed to need the lonely exercise of writing as an outlet—something I can recognize in myself with the passing of time. As I reflect on that year, I see Ray as challenging me to respond to him, to shift my teacher lens, as Deborah Hicks (2002) wrote, from the general context of the classroom discourse to "the particulars of the histories that give shape and meaning to engagements with literacies" (p. 145). Ray seemed to want acceptance, and he found writing as one path through which to gain mine. And the fragments of my interactions with Ray began accumulating on my table without my even knowing it.

TEACHER INQUIRY AND POETRY

For me, as a participant in the Red Clay Writing Project Teacher Inquiry Community, encountering Ray was just what I needed at the time. I agreed to do classroom research—collect data and write about what I learned about teaching in my classroom—and was looking forward to analyzing my students' home to school journals and doing some academic writing about my learning process. I hoped my acute focus would permit me to see Ray differently—as a complex individual, striving "not only for cognitive awareness, but for social belonging and identity" (Hicks, 2002, p. 145). It seemed the perfect way to try something new and write through my attempts at engaging critical pedagogy with a student I perceived as vulnerable in the sometimes unforgiving world of middle school.

Excited about the opportunity to extend myself as a teacher and writer, I was surprised by the firm no I received in response to my request to my school district for conducting classroom research. It was a disappointing blow, perhaps reflective of an era of high-stakes testing and teacher accountability that claims to support "research-based" practices but denies teachers the intellectual position from which to do their own research. A new conundrum emerged: How was I supposed to think and write about my teaching practice (do "teacher research") without institutional approval? And yet on the other hand, the university IRB (Institutional Review Board, for research) that privileges quantitative and experimental design research does not consider poetic inquiry to be research at all. Living between two bureaucracies, both with very different definitions of research that I carry with me in my work as a teacher, I moved forward with writing poetry and asked Ray permission to publish this chapter about him.

My life as a creative writer was flourishing, prompted by graduate coursework in flash fiction and poetry. If I could write flash fiction— short, creative fiction, running about 500 words—about my experiences as a teacher, could I do the same with poems? Didn't the task require the same heightened "attention to the rhythms of speech in communities" (Cahnmann, 2003, p. 31) and heightened awareness of interpersonal relationships and group dynamics? Yes, the exercise of writing poetry and thinking and writing poetry again could lead to what Rebecca Luce-Kapler (2009) called preparation for "serendipity of insight" (p. 75). Writing poetry was the perfect way for me to think deeply about my practice and do creative work at the same time.

While I knew I didn't need administrative approval to write poetry, I did doubt my ability to do the inquiry process justice. It was always important to me to make art through my writing, but I needed it to be credible in my scholarship, too. Elliot Eisner (2008), in describing the persistent tensions in arts-based research, called for "secure technologies of mind that will enable us to peer more deeply into situations that might not be the same as the one we study" (p. 21). This was my demand of poetry. In taking bits of conversation, journal entry, and classroom discussion, I needed my writing to reflect what poet Charles Simic described as an "epistemological and metaphysical problem for the poet" (cited in Zwicky, 2003, p. 2). In other words, I couldn't simply write cute poems about the things Ray said in class. I would have to let these lines of conversation linger in my mind, or rather, place them on a "table," where I might think about what they might mean in a larger context as I went about my day or even week. Then, when I felt ready, I would attempt to make art through what I learned from the experience.

What I wasn't ready for, though, was thinking about myself so critically. Poet and sociologist Laurel Richardson (1992) described poetry writing as an experience that sharpened her critical eyes and ears, enabling her to become more attuned to the lived experiences of others. However, the process had personal impact in that it "affected my willingness to know myself and others in different ways" (p. 135).

One day, after I completed a strand of conversation in our dialogue journals, Ray was on my mind. During our back-and-forth exchange we talked about writing—when we like to do it, where we feel most comfortable and creative. He revealed in this conversation thread that he wrote himself a letter every night. It surprised me, and I questioned him about this practice.

It was calming.

It helped him focus.

The more he answered me, the more I couldn't get the image out of my head. What made a boy so angry, so anxious, or uncertain that he had to calm himself through letter writing every night? I tried to write a poem to make some sense of it.

At Night He Writes

1   On bad days,
    he writes a letter
    to himself. Says
    the writing helps
5   *me focus before*
    I fall asleep.
    What happens
    if you skip a day?
    You don't want
10 *to see that guy.*
    I think about
    that word—focus
    wondering if it
    really means *forget.*

I workshopped the poem among peers, and through the group I heard what I knew but wasn't ready to face. The poem wasn't done; it was just a start. There was more to be said and written than two little stanzas. Toi Derricotte (1997) says, "Sometimes people can't get past what they think they see" (p. 64), and by workshopping the poem I learned that as both a teacher and an emerging poet, I was not ready to move beyond my initial wrestling with the idea of a boy writing himself a letter each night. Perhaps Ray's letter writing was simply the tip of the iceberg, and maybe I needed to ask harder questions of myself and of Ray. For instance, What made him so angry all the time? Why the letter, and why did he feel compelled to tell me about it? Why did his words haunt me so?

"There's a very dangerous moment when feelings, real feelings start to emerge" (Derricotte, 1997, p. 122). In hindsight, I believe that I used my early writing as a shield against what I was trying to understand about Ray. Members of the group encouraged me to write more; they wanted to hear more and know more about Ray. Some thought the piece shouldn't be a poem at all, but rather a flash fiction piece or short story. I rejected that idea. I would think about it, but I would stick to creative nonfiction in poetic form.

Even months later, I did not return to the poem as my group members suggested during workshop. I focused instead on building my student-teacher relationship with Ray. I did continue to write about him and conversations we shared, but I backed off that particular moment of inquiry. Perhaps I was frightened of what he might say and the subsequent response I would have to make. I knew him well enough to know he would demand it if he took the time to answer my initial question.

His words on paper, our conversations and interactions—they were all artifacts scattered upon a table inside my head. The first time I set them on that workspace, I saw them in a certain way, knowing that perception was unlikely to change if I failed to read or reflect further. Although it took a whole year of scooting up to, walking past, dropping new pieces on, and rearranging the piles on that table of knowledge, eventually, I was capable of seeing the "hints of meaning" that Charles Simic described. The work, though, of thinking about past conversations with Ray and writing about those interactions and then revising my work in a never-ending journey toward creating art was imperative for me to see differently. As Cahnmann (2003) wrote, while the demands of writing poetry are great, so is the potential "to make our thinking clearer, fresher, and more accessible and to render the richness and complexity of the observed world" (p. 34).

The same could be said for conducting qualitative research, so it's highly possible I was not as afraid as I imagined myself to be. Perhaps I was in the natural process of inquiry, leaving the poem, fragments of my conversation with Ray, and the interactions that came after it on the back burner, precisely where they needed to wait, breathe a bit, until I had the chance to read writers such as Toi Derricotte and think about how her memoir informed my meaning-making. As it turned out, my poem was "done." It captured my wonder and worry for Ray, and while I wasn't shutting the door on the possibility of revision, I didn't feel guilty about leaving it on the table just as I'd left it a year ago.

But that didn't mean I didn't feel the need to pick up another piece of writing for consideration. The time and thinking space prompted me to revisit my other writing about Ray. In the following vignette, "How to Make Change in Middle School," I tried to help Ray secure change for a $20 bill so he could purchase a school identification card. He needed to get the change quickly because we were headed out that day on a class field trip. To save time, I sent him to our school cafeteria, a place I knew could help.

How to Make Change in Middle School

We're in the middle of field trip "preps"—last minute things such as the lunch question. Will they bring it or buy it? ID cards, too. Students have to have their ID badges when we travel off campus.

Ray still hasn't bought one, and time is running out. He comes to class discouraged the last day out. I put my hands out, palms up, and ask, "So what's the deal?"

"They said they don't have change."

"Well, just go to the cafeteria ladies and ask them for change."

"I told you. They said they don't have it."

"The cafeteria ladies?"

"Yeah."

"Oh. I get it." And I do. The cafeteria ladies are notorious for withholding change when everyone can see the 1s and 5s bulging out of the cash drawer. I have figured out how to get what I need in their strange world, so I decide to pass the knowledge on.

"Ray. Here's what you do. First, you smile. That's important. Then, you ask nicely for a favor and tell them how much you appreciate their help. Next, while you're apologizing for the inconvenience, you reach in your pocket, pull out the twenty—keep smiling—ask please one more time and then start telling them thank you for their help. They'll give you change."

"I can't do that."

"Sure you can."

He shakes his head and slouches in his chair, defeated. I'm discouraged too because I thought he was ready for this next step. In recent weeks I've noticed a sense of empowerment growing in Ray. All positive and exciting. Ray said he wanted to study slavery in America after we finished the Holocaust. Ray recently demanded more difficult vocabulary. He actually said, "I'm way beyond this," waving his hand in disgust at my selections. He would ask to repeat activities he enjoyed. I thought he might be ready to try his skills outside our reading classroom, but I was wrong.

I sigh and get ready to start our lesson, and I'm surprised to see him standing next to me all of a sudden. He holds out a folded-over piece of notebook paper. Taking it from him, I ask if he wants me to read it. He nods. There's a $20 bill inside and one word on the paper— *Pleaze*.

"You want me to do this?" I ask.

He gives me a serious nod, pauses, then adds for good measure, "Bring me the change."

"I wasn't planning on keeping it," I say with a smile. *At least he hasn't forgotten he's entitled to that.*

With fresh eyes, I reconsidered this text and, almost immediately, I could "see" the possibility for something different. The piece, although it was short, seemed laden with unnecessary explanation that in my opinion, weighed down the learning moment I was trying to convey. In order for me to share my insight, it needed to focus on the moment and the moment only. This piece was a poem waiting to happen.

One of the most important lessons I've learned as a teacher and writer is that knowledge is not something we find at the end of a road. We read, we ponder, and we ask more questions along the path. It's part of an ongoing practice, what Cahnmann (2003) referred to as a "critical iterative feedback loop that informs ongoing decision making" (p. 32), and I can't help but believe in the potential of poetic inquiry as I continually attempt to write through my burning questions. What's odd to me is how fixated I become about answering the big questions. I don't really consider the little fires I either put out or start up along the way.

The change-making incident could have been a little fire, but I made it a burning question in that I thought Ray, through his growth in my classroom, where he was demanding more complex material and control over his learning, was ready to stand up and negotiate for himself successfully.

Such was the case with me as well with this piece of creative nonfiction. From a teacher standpoint, I failed to drill down to the particular act of making change and what that meant for Ray in that moment. I also got stuck in narrative form, and as a result, my perception never wavered from the general. I didn't consider the learning possibility for me as the teacher of a disenfranchised student. Poetic inquiry would have given me the chance to study this little oppression and perhaps learn something new through arts-based representation. Reflection brought me back to the table with new eyes, and as I've asked my students to do so many times before, I "found" a poem in my original narrative:

The Time I Tried to Teach Ray the Art of Making Middle School Change

1   My hands are out, palms up—
    Expectant. Did you get it? His face
    falls into a pit of dejection.
    They said they don't have it.
5   They did, huh? The cafeteria ladies—
    Notorious for holding back the cash
    when everyone can see 1s & 5s
    bulging out of their money drawers.
    Hairnet-wearing women wielding
10 micropower over children.
    I sigh just like a teacher.
    Look Ray, it's simple. Go back and—
    Try again. Just smile at them. Hold
    the money out and say thank you, but—
15 Keep smiling. That's so important.
    They will give it to you. He shakes
    his head. *You just don't understand.*
    Okay. Have a seat, Ray. We move
    on to our lesson of semicolons.
20 A moment later, he is next to me,
    holding out a folded note—an offering
    on notebook paper. Opening it, I find
    his $20 covering the single word—*Pleaze.*
    I sigh like a mother and ask—

25 You want me to do this for you? He
    looks at me—hard and serious, yet
    vulnerable, as he gives me a single,
    solemn nod and returns to his seat
    at the back of the room.

Did I capture this moment and make art in the process? I hope so.
Did I get the images just right? Probably not. Will I revisit the poem
over time? Most certainly. For better or worse, it is my nature to over-
think things. My writing is no exception. I'm constantly opening old
notebooks and tweaking lines in poems and short stories, as I never
consider my writing "finished."

Now that Ray has moved on to high school and I don't see and talk
to him every day, I realize how important these exchanges were to our
growing relationship back then. His requests, from help with tying his
tie on game day to advice on how to secure change from the ladies in the
cafeteria, were all seemingly mundane, yet they gave him something.

Certainly, they gave me something, too.

Carl Leggo (2008) wrote, "We need to write personally because we
live personally, and our personal living is always braided with our
other ways of living—professional, academic, administrative, social,
and political" (p. 91). His statement could not be truer of my writerly
and teacherly lives. Richardson (2000) echoed Leggo's words when she
argued that poetic craft allows teacher-researchers to be "more fully
present in our work, more honest, more engaged" (p. 924).

Thoughtful and honest engagement with Ray, starting where we
both were, in our classroom with a single journal entry, presented us
with the potential for positive transformation. Ray gained confidence
to participate in daily life, enough so he told me a year later that he
didn't write nightly letters anymore. "I just don't need it anymore,"
he said. I gained not only the courage to write about my practice but
also the insight required to know that I needed to be flexible in my
teaching and open and willing to change to accommodate the needs of
my students. Through this process of using writing as a tool to become
a better teacher, poetic inquiry enabled me to enact critical pedagogy.

I'd like to believe I participate actively in the ongoing process that
former poet laureate Stanly Kunitz called "letting go and pulling back"
(Kunitz & Moss, 1993, p. 13). The writing, workshop, and revision of
"At Night He Writes" and "The Time I Tried to Teach Ray the Art of

Making Middle School Change" reflected this process in an almost cy-clical model of interaction with text. True, there were pit stops along the way when I stalled and wasn't prepared to listen or think about what a reviewer had said about my poem. However, through reading and thinking and revisiting the lines, I eventually sat down at the table and pushed on toward a new revision.

THE IMPACT OF POETIC INQUIRY

As I reflect on the writing of these single poems, I recognize the impact of the workshop experience on an author in terms of writing process, but when I think about how it influences a classroom teacher conduct-ing poetic inquiry, I am blown away by its power. I can't imagine not having the opportunity to think about my classroom through writing. Certainly, I become a better teacher because I am engaged in the pro-cess, actively using my senses and constantly thinking about what I hear each day, but the real benefit comes from the cyclical nature of the process. If I'm reflecting intently enough about the interactions in my classroom to write them down on paper, then I make a teacherly agreement with myself to think these interactions through in a critical and creative way. I may not ponder them every day, but by placing my thoughts through poetry on a table in my mind, I commit to returning to them one day. As time passes and my classroom experiences inform my point of view, my perspective may change the poem. In this way my thinking about teaching remains fresh and new as I constantly re-vise, and consequently, with the process never ending, I never stop thinking about how to be a better teacher.

However, I don't simply become a better teacher by writing poems; I become a better person as well. At least, the act of writing and then revisiting my words gives me that opportunity. It is a way to share what I learn with others; as Judith Ortiz Cofer (2011) wrote, "By read-ing and writing about what most matters to us, we pass it—what we have learned, what has shaped us into who we are—forward" (p. 86).

The review process is like a mirror, reflecting my attitudes, actions, hopes, and fears. If I'm serious about improving my writing, I have to take a hard look at the words and listen to others talk about how they make them feel. Then I must decide what to do with their construc-tive criticism and revise my work. After that, I return to my classroom, often with fresh perspective and what Cahnmann (2003) called "ever-obsessive ears" (p. 29). From there, I return to my poem with new bits of conversation and understanding to add.

For the true classroom researcher armed with poetic inquiry, the learning never stops. As a writer and researcher, the words of Ruth Behar (2008) ring true for me: "There is poetry to be found in all human endeavors to understand the world. The thing is to know how to see the poetry, how to hear the poetry, how to feel the poetry" (p. 62). I am in my classroom with my notebook, looking and listening for it all the time. I only hope the writer in me is ready to receive it—and I take the time to rework it—and make art.

Guiding Prompts and Questions

1. Allisa uses poetic inquiry—and the making of poems—to notice, write about, and revise what she discerns about her pedagogical interactions. How does the use of poetry change the way you think about this student, teacher, and teaching?

2. How might the practice of writing and revising poetry from the classroom help a teacher cultivate critical pedagogy?

3. Allisa's poems focus on interactions outside the formal curriculum. Why do you think this is so? What insight might this offer teachers who want to have more just relations in their classrooms?

Writing Group Exercise

1. Become a living movie camera in your work as a teacher. Sit in your classroom for several minutes and observe as many sights and sounds as you can. Write these down in specific detail. Later, review what you've written and look for hints of new understanding. Pull out the most powerful details and either write about one or fashion these concrete phrases into the beginning of a poem.

2. Find a poem in a memory. Begin with writing down a memory as specifically as you can. Write it all—what was said, how you felt, where you were, what you wore. This exercise usually yields 2–4 pages of text. Let this writing sit and return to it after several days or weeks. In the same way we may teach students to write found poems, read your text and pull out the powerful phrases and burning questions. Arrange these lines into poetic form, revising your work as needed.

REFERENCES

Behar, R. (2008). Between poetry and anthropology: Searching for languages of home. In M. Cahnmann-Taylor & R. Siegesmund (Eds.), *Arts-based research in education: Foundations in practice* (pp. 55–71). New York, NY: Routledge.

Cahnmann, M. (2003). The craft, practice, and possibility of poetry in educational research. *Educational Researcher, 3*(32), 29–36.

Cofer, J. O. (2011). *Lessons from a writer's life: Readings and resources for teachers and students.* Portsmouth, NH: Heinemann.

Derricotte, T. (1997). *The black notebooks: An interior journey.* New York, NY: W.W. Norton.

Eisner, E. (2008). Persistent tensions in arts-based research. In M. Cahnmann-Taylor & R. Siegesmund (Eds.), *Arts-based research in education: Foundations in practice* (pp. 16–27). New York, NY: Routledge.

Hicks, D. (2002). *Reading lives: Working-class children and literacy learning.* New York, NY: Teachers College Press.

Kunitz, S., & Moss, S. M. (Eds.). (1993). *Interviews and encounters with Stanley Kunitz.* Hanover, NH: Sheep Meadow Press.

Leggo, C. (2008). The ecology of personal and professional experience: A poet's view. In M. Cahnmann-Taylor & R. Siegesmund (Eds.), *Arts-based research in education: Foundations in practice* (pp. 89–97). New York, NY: Routledge.

Luce-Kapler, R. (2009). Serendipity, poetry, and inquiry. In M. Prendergast, C. Leggo, & P. Sameshima (Eds.), *Poetic inquiry: Vibrant voices in the social sciences* (pp. 75–78). Rotterdam, Netherlands: Sense.

Richardson, L. (1992). The consequences of poetic representation: Writing the other, rewriting the self. In Carolyn Ellis & Michael Flaherty (Eds.), *Investigating subjectivity: Research on lived experience* (pp. 125–137). Newbury Park, CA: Sage.

Richardson, L. (2000). Writing. A method of inquiry. In Norman K. Denzin & Yvonna S. Lincoln (Eds.), *Handbook of qualitative research* (2nd ed., pp. 959–978). Thousand Oaks, CA: Sage.

Zwicky, J. (2003). *Wisdom and metaphor.* Kentville, Nova Scotia: Gaspereau Books.

CHAPTER 6

Killing Giants and Critical Pedagogy

Becky Hasty

*In this chapter, high school English teacher Becky Hasty draws on her love
of literature and particularly the graphic novel* I Kill Giants *to craft a personal
narrative about her pedagogical relationship with one of her students,
Phineas. She asks why school is yet another giant in youths' lives rather than
a place of refuge where youth acquire the tools to overcome all the giants
in their lives. The work of a teacher and indeed the meaning of school and
education are both questioned and interrogated through every layer of this
study and in the writing of the chapter.*

SOMEONE IS BEING RUDE

I Kill Giants, a graphic novel by Joe Kelly and Ken Nimura (2009), begins in a classroom. It's 5th-grade career day and Aidan's dad, the motivational speaker, is demonstrating the skills of his trade, how he makes boring into soaring and lame into flame. Ms. Dean, the teacher, has to interrupt though, because someone isn't participating.

Someone is being rude.

Barbara Thorson, the goofy-looking girl in the back row, studies a book intently. Mr. Cooper takes on Barbara's indifferent challenge. As he says, it is his job to take the unmotivated and, using only his words, motivate them. But Barbara isn't impressed by motivating a "room full of losers with no self-esteem out of their money." She has a career; she kills giants.

This sounds like a book about a quirky girl with an overactive imagination, and it is, but Barbara Thorson's giants are not imaginary. They are real, terrifying, and life threatening, and her school offers no help. Barbara is preoccupied with the threat filling her everyday life, and everyone writes her off as silly, rebellious, a troublemaker because she won't fly right, won't forget the giant-killing nonsense and learn the lessons the school deems valuable.

Just like Barbara's school, our schools, which should equip kids with tools to conquer the giants of life, don't often offer such empowering possibilities. Instead, school becomes another giant to confront. Just like the motivational expert pumping the audience's energy, educators often believe we offer students the necessary weapons for a successful future. We don't see that most of the time we provide only indoctrination into our way of believing and behaving.

For the 2009–2010 school year, I was involved with a research project through the Red Clay Writing Project and tried to figure out how to incorporate a social justice thread into the weave of my 9th-grade literature classes. Going into the project, I knew I didn't have a clear idea of what social justice teaching would mean for my students. At the end of the project, after focusing on one student and his relationship to the school and education, I had more clarity on the flaws in my own beliefs and the depth of the challenges faced by my students and our schools.

In 12 years of teaching at the high school level, I have thought a lot about marginalized students and I saw the "problem" of marginalized students mostly in terms of their lacking a strong identity as readers and writers. In other words, I believed that if they would just read and write more—and better—they could be and do anything they wanted. I worked to help my students develop personal motivation to read more, and I tried to connect writing to real-world uses without strangling them with the doctrine of pedantic, prescriptive expository writing that employs elevated, thesaurusized language and tone, very serious as executed by the novice (Romano, 1987).

Prior to the teacher inquiry community project, I had taught literature and composition classes for underprepared high school freshmen for 3 years. That experience taught me the most valuable lesson of all: caring about students—even when they don't do the work and even when they don't care about school, schoolwork, and school success—is imperative. When I learned to develop relationships with a student independent of those issues, my teaching blossomed. I can even believe that a few of the kids who went through those classes with me remained in school in part because they had that one teacher who looked out for them during their 1st year. Certainly, though, I can name many of their classmates who didn't stick around.

I don't think I was completely naive before I began this project with my Red Clay colleagues. I understood that schools reproduce the power structures of our culture. As Lisa Delpit (1995) put it, there is a culture of power with codes and rules that participants must learn in order to be accepted in powerful spaces and to wield their own power in ways that would be deemed appropriate by mainstream society. At the start of the teacher research project I already felt that the American Dream, the democratization of education, and Horatio Alger's bootstraps are all rhetoric produced by our society and educational system that lead us to blame individuals who don't succeed and lead those individuals to internalize the blame for their own lack of success.

In *Literacy with an Attitude*, Patrick Finn (1999) explained that in the United States we have two kinds of education: First "there is the empowering education, which leads to positions of power and authority. Second there is domesticating education, which leads to functional literacy, literacy that makes a person productive and dependable, but not troublesome" (p. x).

I always understood that my students needed an empowering literacy, but in doing this teacher research I realized that my ideas of how to achieve this empowering literacy were indeed naive and inadequate. My year of reflection and study allowed me to really understand the disconnect between what our schools propose to do *for* students and what in fact is done *to* our students.

Phineas—False Starts Against Giants

Just as I entered the project with a sense of knowing that I would discover to be flawed and inadequate, the selection of a focal student defied my intentions. I kept notes on a few students during the 1st semester of classes but didn't really develop a connection with any of them. When Phineas, my final choice, came into the picture he wasn't even in one of my classes at the time.

Phineas entered high school in 2008 and failed all four of his classes in the fall semester as a result of missing more days of school than the rules permitted. In his 2nd semester he missed 34 days of school and failed all four classes again. And in the fall of 2009 he once again failed all four classes because of absences. Before he got on track, Phineas would take each of those freshman classes—lit, science, social studies, and math—three times each.

But it was in that 1st semester of 9th grade lit when I called his mom after a stretch of five absences in a row. She related to me some of the obstacles facing Phineas. Phineas's parents had been together since well before he was born, practically high school sweethearts, but issues of education, substance abuse, and trouble with the law meant that they didn't hold regular jobs and didn't have much besides sincere good wishes to offer toward helping their children succeed in school. In his own words, Phineas acknowledged this:

No one ever really gave me the pushes I need. They still don't. I've always just been told, "Hey, doing good in school will get you far in life." Yeah, sure. The people who tell me this never even graduated high school. All I've ever heard were words to push me forward, but sometimes that's not enough.

His dad was in jail at the time and his mom had no driver's license, no car, and no one to give her a ride to come in and talk to the school authorities. And if Phineas missed the bus (which was classified by the school as an unexcused absence) she had no way to get him to school.

Phineas also experienced social stress through middle school that may have been related to his socioeconomic status. He told me about his best friend in 4th and 5th grade—back when he was in the gifted program—who had been as close as family and whose mother had been like a surrogate parent to him. But the social pressures and course schedules of middle school had brought an end to the friendship. Different teams and schedules drove a wedge between the friends.

That same boy was in the 9th-grade class where I first met Phineas. Even when Phineas's grade was past hope and he had stopped participating in any other way, Phineas always helped that former friend with computer work, cutting and pasting, adding hyperlinks and annotations—all skills Phineas was very competent with and the friend wasn't. At the time, it was not obvious that the two had ever been close friends, but it was evident that they moved in very different circles by that point. Phineas didn't say that money was a factor, but he did describe the former friend's clique as the rich kid group.

So after this gifted student had been forced through summer school to be passed into 9th grade, it should have been apparent that he had both potential and problems. However, nothing besides a permanent folder in the guidance office vault followed him from middle to high school. Nothing was done to inform his 2nd-semester teachers that he had failed all four of his 1st-semester courses. Then, when he began his 2nd freshman year, nothing was passed on, no plans were made, and no air-bags were activated to ensure that his 2nd freshmen year would be anything less than another failure.

For Phineas, an important first lesson of high school was that the deck was stacked against him. If he missed the bus, he couldn't get to school, but that was considered an unexcused absence. For Phineas, this was one more reason to believe that he was not liked and couldn't succeed.

When asked to reflect on barriers to getting an education, Phineas said:

> I cannot go after school or before school to make up things. Right now I have to make up credits for classes; I failed and I have no reliable transportation. Before I would miss a lot of school days. I was failing all my classes. This was because I felt that I had no purpose for education. I had the idea that it's "whatever, I can drop out, do nothing. It'll be okay." I had around 30 absences my freshman year. The only reason I used to go to school was to not get in trouble and to get out of the house so I wouldn't be bored.

So at its best, the education we were offering Phineas up to that point was a domesticating one (Finn, 1999). It was more important that he follow the rules of the school, that he sit in class for the required number of days, than that he was bright and capable and on the fast track to dropping out just as his mother and father and most of his family had done before.

What changed for Phineas? Did the heartfelt intervention of one teacher and the power of reading and writing turn it all around?

Not exactly.

Beginning to Connect in the Land of Giants

The first time Phineas took 9th-grade literature and composition, he was in my class. However, Phineas did very little except sleep during that time. Mr. G, a special education team teacher, was also in the class and had known Phineas since middle school. Mr. G was constantly waking Phineas up and forcing work in front of him. These were the main impressions I had of Phineas in that semester.

The student teacher maintained my practice of making the majority of reading independent and student driven instead of reading assigned books together. So when the class chose independent novels, I got to know Phineas better. On our first shopping trip to the media center, every student selected a book and headed back to class.

But not Phineas.

Phineas's dark hair perpetually falling over his eyes, his slouch, and a well-worn Metallica T-shirt beneath a baggy sweat jacket had familiar echoes of other students in past classes. I took into consideration his demonstrated disinterest in the schoolness of a literature class and suggested *Cirque du Freak* (Shan, 2010), a series that many kids who seemed disengaged in school had been avidly interested in. I learned Phineas had read the whole series already and no other books interested him. However, the topic of vampires led us to discuss my pet obsession, *Buffy the Vampire Slayer* (Whedon, 1996) and to a lesser extent the spinoff show *Angel* (Whedon, 1999).

Angel, it turned out, was one thing Phineas liked a lot. He watched it regularly with his mom. There was one *Angel* novelization in the library, and it just so happened that I had the comic book continuation of the *Angel* series in my room.

I knew we had made a connection. Phineas and I were talking the talk of fandom and I got a glimpse of the sharp, witty kid who was usually played by Sleepy and Surly. I hoped that the connection and the reward of books no one else could provide would motivate his renewed interest in showing his brightness in class.

It had happened before—that brilliant turn-around story of a disengaged student finding her or his inspiration in literature. It could have happened again, and I was hopeful, but that year it didn't happen for Phineas in 9th-grade lit. The turnaround for Phineas wasn't the interest of one teacher and it certainly wasn't something that grew out of the educational system. The big changes began in the 1st weeks of 2010 when he and a younger sister were removed from their home by the police and the department of social services.

More Giants

The night Phineas was removed from his house the police arrived at 3:00 in the morning on a domestic call. It was the 2nd time they had been there within a short period. The adults in the house were reportedly so intoxicated that they couldn't explain who Phineas and his younger sister were, and Phineas was up and playing on a computer despite it being a school night.

I found out about these events almost by accident. There wasn't any real effort made by administrative forces in the school to assist Phineas as his world crashed around him. When I found out, though, I decided to get Phineas placed in my 9th-grade lit class for his third attempt and I also managed to get him in a mythology elective I taught.

Not so ironically, because being placed in a foster home made Phineas homeless, the county was required by law (the McKinney-Vento Homeless Education Assistance Act) to provide transportation for Phineas from his foster home that was outside the county. The administration also agreed to return two credits he had been denied because of absences for classes he had passed his 1st year.

For the next 4 months, Phineas's main focus was on getting back to his home. Despite their shortcomings, he loved his parents and wanted his family reunited. To accomplish that, he focused on following the directives of Family Services, which included finding a mentor. I took on that role, and maybe to please me as well as Family Services, Phineas began to try harder in his classes.

By the next grading period, Phineas was passing all his classes and showing signs of seeing himself differently. He asked me to email his older sister, who lived, without a car, in another county. He wanted her to know how well he was doing in school, earning a 95 in mythology, an 85 in lit, a 92 in law enforcement, and a B in physical science.

His sister replied:

That's fantastic! I've been waiting years to see those grades go back up. Phineas's always been a "trouble maker" kind of student. He always says his teachers "hate him" so he fails.

He really just lacks motivation so teachers assume he's not intelligent. He really loves your class though. Every time I see him he's got a new book, lol. I never thought I'd see that.

Just as his sister said, Phineas had a wealth of talents that school had never motivated him to use or ones that we had caused him to doubt.

Untapped Resources

As we worked together, Phineas's untapped potential began to show with his new motivation. That semester, he read 10 novels independently. He also began attending my after-school writing group. That surprising turn came about because when he stayed I drove him home and took him out for dinner. A Dairy Queen chicken basket and Blizzard were a fabulous treat.

No matter what his reasons for attending the writing group were, Phineas always participated in the writing portion of the meeting. He didn't share his writing aloud with the group, but he always gave me the writing afterward. Once again the results showed that he had all the basic skills necessary—and even the beginnings of an aptitude—for storytelling. The following is Phineas's response to a prompt about a mysterious open door, which he completed in about 30 minutes with no revision:

The door is open because someone was being chased by a giant dragon and they decided to run into the house for cover. The dragon was purple and green, most commonly known as the purple greenback dragon. So when the person gets in the house, he looks around. As he's looking he finds that the house is in fact not a house at all; it's an underground cave with a big, board house disguise over the entrance. So as he's walking, he sees bones everywhere, on the walls, ground, and the ceiling. As scared as he is, he keeps going. The cave seems to not have lighting, but it has this natural glow to it. It's not so bright that you can't see, and not too dark to where you can't see, but it's got just the right glow so that you can see what's around you.

So he keeps walking, and he sees he is coming to an end up ahead. So a couple of minutes later he reaches an end, where he sees a dark crawl hole. He decides to get one of the naturally glowing rocks off

of the side of the cave and look inside the crawl hole. When he looks
into the darkness, he sees something open its eyes. He calls out to
it and gets no answer. Then the eyes are gone. Next thing he knows
something grabs and pulls him into the darkness. Then the thing rips
his right arm off and starts draining the blood out of his body. So as he
is dying, he thinks, "So the dragon chases people into the cave for the
vampire to kill them."

Phineas had all the potential a school could ask for, yet even with a
mentor's help, there are crucial skills he hadn't mastered, tools that we
had not given him. It was obvious that Phineas's reading and writing
skills were well developed, but he saw his school writing quite differently, and I had trouble processing the incongruity. Although he vol-
untarily wrote for the writers' group, he rarely attempted any in-class
writing. As he told me in an email exchange:

> i havent had practice writing. . . . i don't like it so i don't practice
> it.im not good at describing stuff in a paper. . . . id rather get it
> over with as easy as i can and be done.

His perception of himself and school writing usually meant not
doing writing at all. When there was an essay question on a test, as
there is in every subject area, Phineas would do the math to see if he
could achieve a passing grade without the writing. If so, he would skip
it; sometimes he would skip it even if it meant failing.

At first, especially since I knew he could write, I saw Phineas's
aversion to school writing as pragmatism. He did have newfound motivation to pass classes, but there was no motivation to push from C to
B to A. With ten Fs on his transcript, he would never compete for the
HOPE scholarship (a lottery-funded college scholarship in the state of
Georgia) and could not get into a competitive postsecondary school.
Taking a C is actually a pretty reasonable allocation of resources under
those circumstances, although many teachers who used to be the kids
learning and excelling for the "fun" of it didn't see Phineas's logic.

Ms. Hasty Begins to Piece Together a Puzzle

I constantly found myself gathering pieces of the Phineas puzzle
(attendance, foster care, feeling out of place in school, etc.) and one

piece of the puzzle came on a memorable day in our 9th-grade lit class. A student teacher (Ms. B) was working in our classroom and she was attempting to get the students to connect to the poem "A Dream Deferred" by Langston Hughes (2004), which was to be used as a lead-in to the short story "The Baddest Dog in Harlem" (Myers, 2001). All Ms. B was asking for that day was a paragraph from each student explaining some dream that had not come true for them. I found Ms. B standing over Phineas and his buddy Pat explaining again and again the assignment, cajoling, questioning, and prompting in a futile attempt to get them to write. Phineas looked at Pat—another 9th-grade repeater, another kid from the housing projects—and then at me and said, "We don't dream, so we can never be disappointed."

The statement was more than an excuse.

It was truth, a fundamental building block of Phineas's world. In order to complete that "simple" assignment, Phineas had to first imagine a life in which people have dreams of better futures, and he had to feel the agency and authority to write in a completely imaginary perspective.

At the time, though, I didn't see a strong connection between this event and our other class writing, such as on the midterm exam. Ms. B had asked students to compare and contrast characterization in the Disney movie *Mulan* (1998) and an Amy Tan short story. This essay was the entire midterm, so 10% of Phineas's grade was riding on the writing. I believed that the task was completely doable for Phineas. He had read the story and watched the movie; he had listened to the discussion. He had proved to me that he had ample writing proficiency. All he needed to do, in all honesty, was parrot the ideas that had been provided by Ms. B. throughout the teaching unit.

I interpreted it to be an issue of motivation, a stumbling block easily conquered given enough encouragement and confidence-building praise. It took 2 days to cajole Phineas into writing a draft. I told him that it was an excellent first draft, and he told me it was "crappy." Then I gave it back with comments and resources to use for revising. He never did the revising, and because he couldn't carry out the pretense of repeating the points made by the teacher, he ended up with a C in my class by the end of the semester. Still he passed and was finally able to move on.

Prior to this I had recognized a problem with the writing that is taught in our English classes, the implications that the "only notable writing is a literary analysis," and the students' "voices are valued only insofar they echo academese" (House, 2006, p. 5). My idea was that the main problem was students' lacking a purpose for their writing. Obviously, in everyday life, students don't spend much time discussing (in third person) Poe's use of *or* rhyme throughout "The Raven." Yet if they could be given a realistic scenario for this discussion, couldn't they begin to learn the language of power valued by the curriculum? Working with Phineas and seeing him continue to struggle with academic writing helped me to see the problem in a different light.

Ms. Hasty and Phineas—The Reciprocity of Teaching/Learning

On the first day of 11th-grade American lit (another teacher's class), Phineas was given an essay assignment—one of four that would decide whether he passed or failed the class. Yet Phineas didn't write anything that day and when forced to go to academic lunch to make up the assignment, all he did was draw waves on his paper.

This "killer" assignment was a personal essay that seemed perfectly reasonable and fit well with the curriculum that leads to the all-important Georgia High School Graduation Writing Test with its focus on persuasive writing.

For the assignment, the student had to write a college admissions letter. Writing from the perspective of an entering college freshman, he needed to persuade the admissions board that he was the best candidate for their school. The prompt gave the writer several ways to go about this persuasion: He could talk about grades, sports achievements, or personal accomplishments. The first two tasks were clearly impossible for Phineas, yet the final option seemed doable. That option encouraged the student to talk about lessons he or she had learned from any work of literature. Phineas could write about anything, I told him; even the Percy Jackson (Riordan, 2010) series that he had just ripped through offered lessons the college admissions board audience could appreciate.

Talking with Phineas, trying to push him through attempting the writing for the sake of passing American lit, I finally saw clearly. While he could manage to write fluidly and entertainingly about a world of glowing rocks, dragons, and vampires, Phineas, in his 11th year of school, could not imagine writing about a work of literature in the authoritative voice we ask students to adopt. We had told him what to say for years, but he had never gained the confidence to see and accept the fiction of that process. In his eyes, anything he could bring to the conversation was stupid and wrong, and imagining a world where his own words were right was as impossible as imagining himself persuading a college to accept him. We had conquered the problem of motivation to succeed, we had shown that he had proficiency as a reader and writer, but there was still one lesson, the pretense of using the language of power that we insisted on but still couldn't force on him.

Phineas did pass American lit and all his classes for the semester. He went on being successful, but school writing remained a stumbling block; however, now he is out of my hands, and despite a desire to do well, he has struggled. The main motivation he has at the moment is the possibility of graduating with his class if he can make up six credits by June. Still, he has nearly failed three classes because he has not learned how and why to do exactly as he is told. He could not simply repeat everything the teacher said about Kate in *Taming of the Shrew* or Nick in *The Great Gatsby*. He did, however, figure out that he enjoys doing creative painting projects to earn that bit of extra credit needed to pass.

Now, his main goal is to work in two semesters of ROTC before graduation then to go on to the air force. I would like to dream that he has the option of college, since he is smart enough and it's hard for me to resist the notion that a diploma can be a ticket to the elusive "American Dream," but truthfully, I think about the first semesters of college—all the studying and writing that is done just for the sake of studying and writing, the need for a facade of expert knowledge—and I know he might be unsuccessful in a very damaging way.

A Changing Giant—New Ways of Domesticating?

In the meantime, some attempts have been made within the school system to prevent repetitions of Phineas's story. Because math scores are our school's current obstacles to Adequate Yearly Progress (as required by No Child Left Behind), funds became available to try small, 15 and under, Math I classes, however, the other freshmen classes are the normal 30 plus and maintained the typical level of failures. Also, repeaters in Math I have been put together in small classes and the same students remained together with the same teacher through Math IV. Phineas was a successful part of this experiment.

The good news and bad news is that for the future, students like Phineas won't be repeatedly scheduled into the same failed classes over and over again, with an ever increasing probability for giving up and dropping out. Instead, our high schools now offer extensive opportunities for computer-based credit recovery before and after school. Students can also use the program to make up units of work in their current courses. Funding even became available to offer transportation in the afternoons. Added to that, there is transportation for summer credit recovery with breakfast and lunch provided. All these options became available this year. There are definitely both pros and cons related to our current credit recovery program.

The computer-based option is a less than ideal substitute for active, engaged learning experiences. With the computers, students listen to prerecorded minilectures then take quizzes and tests over the lecture material. Before they submit their answers, a certified teacher-facilitator checks their work and flags the wrong answers so the student can go back and correct mistakes. This process goes on until the student completes a sufficient percentage of the work with a sufficient average.

In the best case, students are not provided with constructive feedback that might help shape their understanding. In the worst case, rather than listen to the lessons, students are playing games, surfing the Net, and doing social networking. It's easy to open up other windows and Google for answers. They don't have to have any understanding of the content in order to get credit for the material.

Our computer-based credit recovery system allowed 75 seniors to be added to the list of graduates in the last weeks before school ended this year, and it is a major factor motivating Phineas to push through another year of school. Yet in the end, all this new system provides is a streamlined version of the same domesticating education. The successful student learns that it is more important to behave and achieve the appearances—passing scores and a list of passed courses—than to gain demonstrable skills or the authority of expertise or the agency to take control of their own lives.

In my own practice I have to separate the general from the particulars. Focusing on just one student, it is easy to get lost in the particulars of what he or she needs, what can be done for just him or her. I can spend hours helping one student write a paper. I can shoot an email to the teacher in whose class he or she is having trouble, and I can give him or her a ride home when he needs to make up work. In short, I can provide the framework for success that a more middle-class background would have given the student about whom I am concerned.

Yet Phineas has a little sister who has already been held back twice so that she is 13 and in the 6th grade. Then there is Pat, who shared my class with Phineas and who failed that year when he stopped attending, then was back the next year to try again. I think of an endless list of other students with the same kinds of issues who have passed through my classroom before and after Phineas. I continue to work daily on constructing a practice that can offer them the empowering education, practice that can lead them to demand to be taught the language and practices of power.

I do my best to get them reading, thinking, writing, and speaking in ways that are engaging and useful and that bridge to the skills they have to have to "succeed."

Daily, I asked students to read texts and have them write about their connections to the reading. I hope that step by step they will learn to experience everything they read through a filter of personal experience and authority. I am also working to incorporate debate throughout the class as a way to lead students to speak as experts on issues they read and write about. Finally, I work to help other teachers in my school and department consider how they teach and how much of what they insist is crucial may be alien and inaccessible to their students, how much is just "Learn this" and "Do this" because it is "what must be done to pass."

For now, though, no matter what I do, my 9th-graders continue to be a part of a system that focuses on domesticating them, not empowering them in ways that make sense for both their present and their future. And far too often teachers are also domesticated in this system, sticking to rules and teaching practices that are meant to "manage" students rather than look closely at, and learn about, students. Both the content of the curriculum and the teaching/learning strategies as well as institutional policies all worked against Phineas. For so long, Phineas didn't see the importance of the curriculum, was allowed to disengage from the teaching/learning practices, and was persistently put at a disadvantage by policies that always work against low-income youth without access to resources. And he didn't have anyone to guide him through the sacred "mysteries" of success. Still, Phineas and other students like him may pass as a result of the option of computer-based credit recovery. Then they can forget the facts embedded in the irrelevant curriculum as quickly as they "learned" them; but they can at least earn a credential that might open other doors for their future lives.

KILLING GIANTS

Phineas and all the students like him face many giants. Just as Barbara
Thorson found, these giants are Titans—forces of nature, inescapable.
Conquering them means learning to live with the power they wield
over life and death. What has the school done to help Phineas in this
struggle? What will they give him besides a piece of paper?

By the end of *I Kill Giants*, Barbara has come to terms with her
giants. She is happy and well adjusted. We see her on the 1st day of
a new school year. She is still encamped behind a book in the back of
the room, but this book is something happy and girly and acceptable,
nothing to do with giants.

The teacher, Ms. Potts, asks the predictable "How did you spend
your summer?" icebreaker, and Barbara talks about her epic battle. Ms.
Potts responds, "Super, just super," and moves to the next name without blinking or missing a beat. School still has no relevance for Barbara.
The only thing that has changed in their relationship is that Barbara
now sits quietly, causing no trouble, while the school ignores the conflicts of her life. The similarities to Phineas are eerie. Indeed, Phineas
has made progress in domesticating himself and navigating the complexities of making it out of high school, but it still has no relevance for
him, and the school continues to ignore the conflicts between his life
and institutional requirements.

Guiding Prompts

1. Notice the way Becky crafts this chapter to create alignment between the
   tone of the graphic novel, the tone of Phineas, her tone as narrator, and
   insights educators can glean from literature and adolescents. How might
   this influence the way you perceive the students in your classroom setting?
2. What do your disengaged students have to teach you? What is required
   of you to hear and learn those lessons?
3. How much of what you do or teach is done because you "have to"? How
   much of that does more to teach students to submit to authority than
   provide them with valuable skills and autonomy to do what they need to
   do?
4. As you read, notice where Becky inserts critique of unjust policies
   and practices as well as where she attempts to enact what she calls
   "empowering education." Where do you see "empowering education"
   happening in your classroom or school?

Writing Group Exercise

In this chapter the reader gets the sense of a young adolescent being beaten down by giant obstacles over which he has no control. Write about a time when you felt powerless, when you were unable to control the circumstances that were affecting your life. Where were the escape routes from that despair? Were adults, peers, literature, art, media, or other pathways out important to you? What can educators learn about their crucial role in helping young people cultivate tools that will ward off some of the giants they will face in life? Imagine an empowering education in your classroom.

REFERENCES

Delpit, L. (1995). *Other people's children: Cultural conflict in the classroom.* New York, NY: The New Press.

Finn, P. J. (1999). *Literacy with an attitude: Educating working-class children in their own self-interest.* New York, NY: State University of New York Press.

House, J. (2006). *Writing is dialogue: Teaching students to think (and write) like writers.* Norwood, MA: Christopher-Gordon.

Hughes, L. (2004). A dream deferred. In *Timeless voices, timeless themes gold level* (p. 904). Upper Saddle River, NJ: Prentice Hall.

Kelly, J., & Nimura, M. K. (2009). *I kill giants.* Berkeley, CA: Image Comics.

Bancroft, T., & Cook, B. (Directors) & Coats, P. (Producer). *Mulan* [DVD]. (1998). Burbank, CA: Walt Disney.

Myers, W. D. (2001). *145th Street: Short stories.* New York, NY: Laurel Leaf.

Riordan, R. (2010). *Percy Jackson and the Olympians Hardcover Boxed Set.* New York, NY: Hyperion.

Romano, T. (1987). *Clearing the way: Working with teenage writers.* Portsmouth, NH: Heinemann.

Shan, D. (2010). *The Cirque Du Freak Collection.* New York, NY: Little Brown.

Whedon, J. (Executive Producer). (1996). *Buffy the Vampire Slayer.* United States: Warner Brothers.

Whedon, J. (Executive Producer). (1999). *Angel.* United States: Warner Brothers.

CHAPTER 7

From Pledging Allegiance to *Your* Flag to Sharing Beignets

Call-and-Response as Critical Pedagogy

Angela Dean and Dawan Coombs

In this chapter, high school English teacher Angela Dean and researcher Dawan Coombs write about their collaborative inquiry into one of Angela's student's classroom experience across a year. They develop the metaphor of call-and-response to make sense of the complex interactions between Angela and her student Antoine. In their argument that teachers should attempt to recognize all the verbal and nonverbal responses of their students in order to understand the way students are engaging, they also make the point that a call-and-response approach to teaching opens up a possibility for critical pedagogy that invites students and teachers to evolve their personal agency.

The crackling noise of a deteriorating sound system signals the daily announcements as a nameless, faceless voice commands, "At this time, let us take a moment to reflect on our day, our purpose, our responsibilities, and what we hope to accomplish [1 minute pause]. Please stand for the Pledge." The students, some in a sleepy haze, reluctantly stand. The nameless, faceless voice begins, "I pledge allegiance . . ."

Antoine: I pledge your allegiance . . .
Speaker: . . . to the flag . . .
Antoine: . . . to the flag . . .
Speaker: . . . of the United States of America . . .

Antoine: . . . to your United States of America . . .
Stephen: Yeah, that's right.

Dawan, a researcher in Angela's first-period literature class, overheard this exchange between Antoine and the intercom speaker—an exchange that may not be very different from those in other classrooms across the country. Seemingly pithy or apathetic remarks from teenagers are not a new phenomenon to high school teachers, or to observers in their classrooms. But Dawan was an observer in Angela's classroom specifically invited to note possible points of connection with Antoine—a student who might be perceived as vulnerable in many ways but powerful in others. Angela was looking for openings to dialogue with Antoine. Overhearing Antoine's comments during the Pledge of Allegiance raised questions for Dawan about how his teacher could overcome the gap between Antoine's perception that whatever was symbolized by the American flag, the Pledge of Allegiance, and even the United States of America, and his perception of where he belonged.

Examining exchanges such as this between Antoine and his environment offered us (Dawan and Angela) the opportunity to look for entry points into dialogue with marginalized students who might not typically engage in school. In this chapter we look at how the data collected across 1 year about Antoine suggests possibilities for encouraging participatory relationships between teachers and students. Our writing weaves together snippets from Angela's teacher research journal, Dawan's observations, interviews conducted between Angela and Antoine, and dialogue journal entries by Angela and Antoine. Whether those exchanges came in the form of words or silences, illuminating them allowed us to explore ways that Angela and Antoine dialogued with one another and the impact of these dialogues on Antoine's academic performance. We hope that looking at both the verbal and non-verbal replies of both Angela and Antoine, as well as gestures and the use of classroom space, will allow readers to consider the possibilities of participatory relationships with students where it may seem that no possibilities for dialogue currently exist. In fact, we argue that approaching teaching through a call-and-response interaction pattern in the classroom—including non-verbal calls and responses—was the key to opening up a critical space where a marginalized young person could move him- or herself into the center of classroom activity.

THE ORIGINS OF THIS INQUIRY

As a part of her involvement in the Red Clay Writing Project Teacher Inquiry Community (TIC), Angela wanted to look closely at the way students from marginalized populations were defined at her school. Having taught in the same school and district for the past 8 years, Angela was aware of how easily marginalized students were lost in the sprawling suburban high school with a population of just under 4,000 students. Additionally, Angela's school district had just eliminated vocational track classes from the school's offerings in an effort to make all students college bound. Although this move by the district was a well-intentioned effort to remove the negative labels and stereotypes associated with vocational tracks, it also ignored the unique needs of this particular group of students. Students in the vocational track had previously benefited from smaller class sizes, individualized attention, and a pragmatic approach to academic engagement; under the new system all students were enrolled in college-prep classes. Angela was concerned about the way her students who seemed to need the most attention and help might get lost in the masses. Their voices were not always heard in the larger school space, and the removal of this track seemed to make it easier to miss the needs of these students among the larger classes of the college-prep track.

As Angela posted her observations to the TIC project wiki, discussed her students in the TIC meetings, and raised questions about this new situation, she realized selecting one of these students would be the focus of her yearlong inquiry. Drawn to Angela's concerns because of her own experiences in the classroom with seeming disengaged youth, Dawan was eager to help with her research. What resulted was a collaboration seeking to discover how to bring out the voices of marginalized students in Angela's college-prep classes.

AN INTRODUCTION TO ANTOINE

Angela ultimately chose to conduct a case study around Antoine. Case study research allows researchers to catch an in-depth look at a phenomenon and the particular contexts that surround it (Yin, 2009). This case study focuses on the transactions between Antoine, his teacher Angela, and his environment.

As a 10th-grade student in a large suburban high school in a mid-sized southeastern city, Antoine posits himself as an outsider to the dominant school culture, but he struggles with also wanting to be part of that culture. The school serves a predominately White population with close to 3,800 students and sits in the middle of several upper-middle-class swim and tennis communities where most of the citizens commute into the city center for work each morning and return home each evening. Students walk the halls before school in the morning, ears plugged with earphones. Most of the cords from the headphones lead to the newest version of an iPod or MP3 player on the market. Students simultaneously text message and carry on conversations while navigating the narrow corridors. Waves of conversations rise and fall, some in various languages or accented voices. The relatively privileged community, though not immune to the economic slump of the past several years, stands in stark contrast to Antoine's life before arriving at Summerville High School.

In 2008 Antoine and his family relocated from New Orleans, leaving behind their home in the Ninth Ward as a result of Hurricane Katrina. They were able to get out of the city before the storm hit, but they lost everything they weren't carrying with them at the time. Antoine describes his life in New Orleans as very different from life in his new community. Neighbors in the Ninth Ward knew one another and constantly crossed paths, but neighbors in the new neighborhood hardly ever interact in either good or bad ways. Antoine spent his time in his old neighborhood outside playing, going to the corner store, and forming his understanding of what he calls "street smarts."

Antoine's evaluations of his school in New Orleans and his new school in Summerville illustrates the value he places on education. He told us, "I like it out here, schoolwise, challengewise, like I feel like I'm learning something. Out there, I felt like we were mostly doing the same thing most of the time."

There are times, however, that he feels some teachers in Summerville do not expect much from him. He states, "I have had people that like talk down upon me, cause I am of my ethnicity and where I'm from and everything. It seems like every teacher wants to talk down to me, I mean I know I'm from an area like that but I'm pretty smart, and when I show them that I'm smart and then they are like, 'Oh, why aren't you acting like . . . ?' And I'm sort of like, 'I don't know.' I don't really feel like I have to prove myself to nobody, so I can just be me, you know, be me." In other words, Antoine understands that the suburban middle-class community in which he lives can offer him access to things the Ninth Ward could not, but he is also painfully aware of stereotypes Summerville folks may hold about him—a fact that may influence his decision to not prove himself to those in power.

FINDING THE CRITICAL PEDAGOGY IN ANGELA'S CLASSROOM

Bakhtin (1993) tells us that language lives in an environment heavy with meaning, where speakers orient their words "toward the listener and his answer" (p. 280). In other words, language isn't objective or neutral, but rather always oriented toward a particular person and the anticipation of how that person might respond. The response of the listener in any given exchange, then, becomes key in shaping the dialogues that take place in everyday life, as well as in any speaker's future goals and interpretations of the other person. If we begin to speak to a person who has treated us poorly in the past, our language is used in a way that might anticipate more poor treatment—thus, an interaction we have today may influence the way we interact with the same person in the future. This proves particularly true in classrooms where teachers and students engage in exchanges of words, ideas, and understanding.

The words teachers and students speak in dialogue are part of a back-and-forth negotiation of meaning-making about academic content, about one another, and about what it means to be successful in the classroom. In a way, Antoine's comments and gestures described in the introduction to this chapter reminded us of the call-and-response traditions of the South, particularly among African American congregations. In these exchanges the speaker's statements or "calls" are affirmed or agreed with in the "response" from the listener through repetition of the calls or through spontaneous talk (Foster, 2002). Antoine's comments and reactions in the classroom followed this pattern, riffing on the original in both tone and meaning.

In traditional call-and-response exchanges, the speaker and the listener are both heard, contributing to a dialogue of sorts through ongoing transactions. Not all these transactions include words, some seem most notable for their silences, but all serve as the basis for ongoing understandings and what might become future dialogues. bell hooks

(2009) reminds us that "hearing each other's voices [and] individual thoughts . . . makes us more acutely aware of each other . . . 'to look at'—each other [and] engage in acts of recognition with one another (p. 139). As teachers and teacher educators working to create critical, dialogic classroom environments that value and include everyone as full participants, paying close attention to our own calls and responses in the classroom as well as our students' calls and responses become key.

What do these ideas mean for educators trying to create classrooms that are engaging and meeting the needs of typically marginalized young people? In this chapter we use the metaphor of call-and-response both as a way to examine the "dialogues" taking place and as a lens to view the oftentimes seemingly nonparticipatory classroom performance of Antoine. We hope that readers might be able to start recognizing the call-and-response rhythms of their own classrooms and ask themselves when they and their students are "more acutely aware of each other" and when they—students and teachers—"engage in acts of recognition with one another." We believe it is in these moments of full awareness and recognition that critical connections are made between teacher, student, and a school environment.

CALLS AND RESPONSES

In this section we examine a few call-and-response exchanges between Angela and Antoine, and we see how Angela's "calls" are met by Antoine's "responses," and similarly how Antoine's "calls" are met by Angela's "responses." Whether those calls and responses come in the form of words or silences, illuminating these exchanges allowed us to explore ways that Angela and Antoine recognized one another and engaged in dialogues, as well as the impact of these interactions on Antoine's academic performance.

First Friday: An Excerpt from Angela's Teacher Research Journal

We have been in school for a week and the kids have made it to Friday. I've made it to Friday. This is an accomplishment. As we head to the library to find choice reading books, I notice Antoine is dressed in his finest jeans, crisp new white T-shirt with a red and brown slogan printed in raised lettering across the chest, and matching tennis shoes and is carrying a brand-new baseball cap. He settles into a chair in the instructional area. A gold necklace hangs from his neck and the gold disk hanging from it has a small diamond attached.

The stack of books I want him to head toward is purposefully at his back. He is not going to find a book to read, because he, as he told me in the classroom before we left, does not read . . . Antoine, unlike the other students dispersed throughout the library, isn't budging from his chair.

As I make my way back to the front of the library, I see that Antoine is still sitting, but now it is as if he's holding court. He has a group of girls sitting and standing around his table. I also see that Mr. Lee, a frequently requested substitute, is there talking with Antoine. Mr. Lee stands and looks Antoine in the eyes. Antoine sits, briefly making eye contact, then looks away, talking more to the group of girls than to Mr. Lee. I'm nervous. Antoine's voice seems to be raised and his posture tells me that he'd rather talk to anyone other than this man.

I take a seat next to Antoine and listen to Mr. Lee's comments. Mr. Lee knows Antoine from last year. He asks Antoine if he remembers their agreement. If Antoine sticks to high school and graduates, Mr. Lee will buy him a Rolex. Every 4 years, Mr. Lee makes this agreement with one student and when that student finishes school, he holds true to his promise. Antoine's tone is light but dismissive. Mr. Lee tries to bait him again and again with the idea of getting a Rolex. Antoine's response is that he'll buy his own. I sit uncomfortably, worried about where this interaction might lead. Thankfully, the bell rings and Mr. Lee, who seems to be totally unfazed by Antoine's attitude about the offer, says good-bye and heads out the door. I tell them to have a good weekend, Antoine gets up, pushes in his chair, and is absorbed into the crowded hallway.

In working with Antoine, I (Angela) saw that he was fully aware of the dominant cultures in which he maneuvered. In his interaction with Mr. Lee in the library, I could see that others recognized Antoine as a student on the fringe. While Mr. Lee's assumptions about guaranteeing a Rolex to students he thought were at risk of not graduating made me uncomfortable, I could not help but feel some validation in my perspective of Antoine as someone indeed on the margins in school. As we made our way to the library that first Friday of school, I asked Antoine about his weekend and what he was looking forward to doing. It was then that I began to understand more about his life outside school and what mattered to him. I learned that he was one of the older children at home and had the responsibility of looking after his younger siblings after school. He was originally from New Orleans, but left when Hurricane Katrina hit the coastline of Louisiana and his home and neighborhood were destroyed. I had a sense that there was more to Antoine than he offered in this brief conversation, and over the course of the year, I worked to find ways to bring him out of his guarded exterior shell by doing my best to be open to seeing and hearing him when he was ready to share.

Choice Reading Day: An Excerpt from Angela's Teacher Research Journal

Antoine comes into class and sits in his seat. It is as far away from my desk and the rest of the class as he can possibly be and still be in the room. The majority of the class sits in the main grouping of desks that face the board . . . A White student who sits in the back corner of the room joins Antoine. They have struck up an unlikely friendship and seem to enjoy making comments to one another that the rest of us cannot hear.

A few minutes in and Antoine has no book and has not shown interest in pulling a book from my bookcase loaded with young adult novels about 5 feet away from his desk. I hop down from my chair and search the shelves for a book that might interest him . . . I pull a few titles from the shelves and stack them on his desk. I don't say anything to him, but instead make my way back to my seat and my book. After about 15 minutes, I ask the students to record their page numbers and we move on to the next activity.

After the bell rings, I scan the room to see what needs to be picked up before my second period arrives. I see two of the three books I pulled from the shelf for Antoine left behind. I walk over and I see that *Monster* (Myers, 2004) is missing.

Although this is an early example of the nonverbal exchanges Antoine and I had over the course of the year, it illustrates how we worked to negotiate the need for Antoine to meet classroom expectations without publicly highlighting his disengagement from assignments. I could have called Antoine out in front of the classroom because he did not have the materials he needed for the day's activities. His outright refusal to look for a book the Friday prior and his lack of following directions again just days later would certainly put off some teachers and even inspire a power struggle that might last the full year. Sensing that putting Antoine in such a position might cause irreparable damage to the relationship I hoped to form with him, I opted to bring as little attention to the exchange as possible. Antoine could have chosen to defy my silent request and refused to choose a book, much less take one with him.

But instead we had successfully started our call-and-response interactions.

Philosopher and literary theorist Mikhail Bakhtin (1981) wrote, "Understanding comes to fruition only in the response" (p. 282), but when students seem unresponsive in the ways that we as teachers seek feedback, it becomes difficult to feel as if any understanding is occurring at all. However, as both Dawan and I learned from Antoine, being open to students' multiple forms of response allowed us—and may allow other teachers—to reach students who seem initially resistant or unresponsive in the traditional forms.

Much like call-and-response, these dialogues are exchanges where one speaker, either by solicitation or spontaneously, calls to the other. The response, whether verbal, nonverbal, musical or physical, acknowledges the words of the other (Foster, 2001). These meanings and understandings revolve around not just content but also the individuals' identities. Besides the flux of ideas that take place as different people exchange ideas, identities exist in a state of flux as well. Our understandings of ourselves are connected to the understandings and perceptions of those around us, of those with whom we are in dialogue. Working toward understanding engages teachers and students in attempts to make meaning of another's words and discern the other's intentions, as ultimately another's identity.

Rogers (2004) states, "Learning involves changes in participation and the subsequent shifts in identity. Such changes construct and are constructed by social change or social transformation. . . . As people interact with the texts of social practices, they are involved in a process of meaning making" (p. 247). The process of making meaning also requires a shift in our ways of interacting, ways of representing, and ways of being while engaging in social practices, all of which are dependent upon how we see ourselves and how others see us. If given the opportunity, I felt, Antoine would take on a new identity in the classroom that looked very different from the ways he generally interacted with school.

Dawan's First Observation of Antoine

Antoine is an interesting kid. I intentionally took a seat near him on the side of the room with a few boys who seemed only slightly but very purposely withdrawn. He wasn't combative, but he did have an "I'm not going to just buy in to what you tell me automatically" sense about him. He listened to the teacher but offered muffled comments in response to her queries too quiet for her to hear. I, however, did hear, and I was fascinated. They weren't disrespectful or rude, but when Angela would ask questions like "Where does the subject go?" in reference to a grammar lesson, he would respond, "I don't know, what do you think?" It was almost like he was talking his way through her lesson, engaging himself in a private dialogue with the teacher, even though her responses were directed to the rest of the class.

This description of my (Dawan's) first observation of Antoine represented one of the first very literal examples of Antoine "dialoging" with Angela, even though she didn't literally hear what he said. He did not meet her words with simply a silent response, but found a way to engage, even if it was not in the traditional sense of classroom participation. Initially his words appeared combative; if he had said these things within earshot of a more authoritarian teacher, the tone of his comments may have been questioned. However, because Angela focused more on the engagement itself, rather than trying to judge whether or not Antoine was threatening her authority, she viewed this as a step toward dialogue instead of as a challenge to her as the teacher in the classroom.

Throughout the rest of the class period I watched as Antoine responded to Angela's queries in a similar manner. But just as in any other exchange, without observation and effort, "the complexity, intricacy, and multifaceted dimensions of any interaction, including the communicative patterns of call-and-response, may remain undetected" (Foster, 2001, p. 295). For example, later, when they began reading and discussing a book, he didn't chime in during discussions, but based on his body language and side comments he seemed to be listening to all of it. He plugged one ear into his iPod buds but was still participating in his "I'm acting like I don't care but I really do" sort of a way. As

Angela mentioned something about being from Georgia, I glanced his way and Antoine said to me, "New Orleans!" with a little hometown pride in his voice. Although it may not have been the ideal response, it offered signs of dialogue with both me and the teacher, and some hope for future engagement.

An Excerpt from a Dialogue Journal Between Angela and Antoine

Angela: What is your relationship like with the [art] teacher you got the detention with? You've told me before that you only really like LA and Spanish. Why is that? How does the rest of your day go? What do you wish your other classes were like?

Antoine: I like LA and Spanish not because of the subject but because of the teachers. Their [*sic*] fun, nice, and I feel relaxed in their class. The rest of my day goes ok. Nothing to brag about.

Antoine's indifference about the subjects of his two favorite classes is telling. He doesn't look forward to attending the classes because he has a vested interest in the content, but because of the atmosphere and the way he feels when he is in the class. It appears that it is more important to him to feel connected personally to the teachers than to the actual subject matter. His choice of the word *relaxed* seems significant here; he seems to want to enter a space where he can feel he doesn't have to worry about being on the defensive—or maybe that he has to "prove" himself to anyone.

Dialogues About Power and the Need for Response

What became evident to Angela from dialogues in the classroom was that Antoine needed to participate in exchanges, verbal and non-verbal, that validated who he was and who he wanted to be. Although he said he didn't feel he has anything to prove, he does want his actions and experiences to matter and to be valued. This became more evident when the class was reading and discussing *Oedipus the King*. This following excerpt was taken from Angela's research journal:

[Antoine's] been good about participating in our discussions on Oedipus. Last week I posed a question about when we look to leaders. I asked them if we looked to leaders in times of prosperity or in times of catastrophe. They all seemed to be in agreement that we look to leaders more often in times of catastrophe and need. They felt that we needed our leaders to guide us and to help us see that the problems could be solved. I then asked them if we were quick to blame leaders when their action or lack thereof failed.

Antoine was ready to talk about how leaders had failed. I asked him for an example and he shared his views of what happened with Hurricane Katrina. He shared briefly about how they waited for days for the government to act and by the time they did, their home had been completely destroyed and was now gone. This got the room talking and then several kids were voicing other ideas. The discussion turned into small sets of conversations around the room, so Antoine was off the hook from sharing more from his experience. I was glad that he shared, but wanted him to expand more on his response. He will do that if I push him a bit. I think he likes to feel invited into our conversations or to feel that we really want to hear him.

My observations about Antoine needing to feel invited into our classroom discussions rather than forced into them speaks to his need to be validated. In this case, he shared from personal experience and felt comfortable enough to make critical statements about one of the most powerful structures of all, our government. The little bit that he shared shaped the dialogue of the classroom. His voice brought in other voices and while those voices eventually took over, they might not have spoken at all had he not articulated his critique of leaders. What could be seen as a challenging question, possibly even threatening, since there is no way of knowing what direction the students might take the conversation, allowed for Antoine to state his views. His participation in whole-class discussions increased over the course of the year where his voice and his experiences were important. Validations from his peers and from myself were integral to his evolution in the classroom. This was not a linear progression, however; there were always days when Antoine would again perform some of the behaviors that were prevalent during the 1st few weeks of school.

Constructing Identity in the Classroom

Antoine's construction of self and participation in the classroom ebbed and flowed throughout the year. One particular example was during the class study of reading Nikki Grimes's (2002) *Bronx Masquerade*. The following is an excerpt from Angela's teacher research journal:

Last week, we came back to one particular poem from the book by [the character] Devon Hope . . . "Bronx Masquerade." He writes, like a lot of kids do, about his identity and being stereotyped. His message, though, is that he wants to take off the mask he's been wearing and show people who he really is. It is a huge step for him to then take this poem and read it to his peers in class. [As a response to this reading in our class] we talked about masks and why people may mask their true identities. I asked them to think of times they had worn "masks" in their lives and why they felt they had to wear them. I asked them if masks were worn based on the groups they associated with, if it was easier to wear masks to avoid judgment, and if it was easier to wear the masks placed upon them by others than to reveal who they really were. Many of them felt it was easier to remain who others felt them to be than to be who they really are or to challenge them.

I asked the students to journal and I noticed that Antoine had his head down and wasn't writing. I walked over to see what was going on with him. When I asked him about the journal he said that he didn't really understand what we were talking about and writing about. He felt that his identity was straightforward and that he didn't really hide who he was at any point in his life.

I wanted them to think about ways they could decorate/illustrate the front to make it address the masks they hid behind and use the back to represent who they really were. Antoine spent the rest of the time in class pulling out pictures of beautiful women from *JET* magazine. I asked him how they might represent who he was, and he just shrugged and laughed.

Freire and Macedo (1987) argued that "pedagogy becomes critical when an educator . . . has a dialogue with students and methodically challenges them to discover that a critical posture necessarily implies the recognition of the relationship between objectivity and subjectivity" (p. 48). In my approach that day I asked students to look critically at the way they were positioned as objects or as agents in terms of the stereotypes that were associated with the various facets of their identities. I knew that Antoine had a critical sensibility, since he demonstrated it frequently, including in his contribution in the *Oedipus* discussion.

However, he did not assume a critical stance when I asked him to think critically about his own identity. I didn't understand why he was being resistant to thinking critically about his identity at this point in the year.

A Telling Dialogue About Technology:
Dawan's Second Observation of Antoine

My second observation in Angela's class included a crucial conversation between Angela and Antoine. As the class worked through drafts of their culture projects, which required them to create a Voicethread project incorporating words, images, and ideas that represented their culture to present to the class, Angela and I wandered around the room, troubleshooting technology concerns and helping students work through the drafting process.

Angela mentioned to me before class began that in previous class periods Antoine had demonstrated a noticeable reluctance to work on this assignment. As we began attending to individual students, both of us wondered if Antoine would be a challenge on that day. In my fieldnotes I wrote:

Antoine definitely had trouble pulling up his assignment; he told me he doesn't use email, so retrieving his username and password were tricky, primarily because he couldn't remember his email address. He eventually got the hang of the Internet skills necessary for this assignment, but there's still no doubt he is behind. When Angela checked in with him during work time and asked if he was working he just said "no."

As I watched, so much hinged on Angela's reaction to Antoine at this moment. If she yelled at or chastised him for not working, her response would seemingly be justified; he was supposed to be working and he wasn't. However, this kind of authoritarian response from other teachers had not yielded positive or compliant reactions from him in the past.

I watched Angela respond to this moment of disconnect as if his response represented a legitimate attempt at the back-and-forth process of meaning-making dialogic teachers engage in with students—the inherent invitations of call-and-response. Angela asked him, "Why?" instead of making assumptions about why and launching immediately into a lecture. As she pressed the issue, Antoine began talking about the technology issues described above. He also explained he hadn't emailed any pictures of his home or traditions because he didn't have any; they had been lost in the hurricane.

Although asking a question like "Why?" took little effort, it revealed much. Antoine's failure to do the assignment had less to do with disengagement than with issues of access to technology, technological practices, and personal access to the required materials representing his "culture." When Angela dialogued with him about these concerns, together they found ways to work through them. He and I googled information about New Orleans and found pictures of his street from the Old Ninth Ward on the Internet. Ultimately by working through these concerns with Antoine we all found ways for him to meet the guidelines for the assignment without taking away requirements or rigor.

The potential hazards of a silent response from Angela at that time seem clear. In a context where utterances and individuals naturally seek understanding and response, "for the word (and, consequently, for a human being) there is nothing more terrible than a lack of response" (Bakhtin, 1986, p. 127). Students who have continually been met with a lack of response by the dominant school culture answer in kind. But for both sides, even this silence represents a type of response. If she had left Antoine alone, he most likely would have remained frustrated and unable to work on his assignment, ultimately failing at this task. Similarly, his refusal to work may have painted him as disinterested and noncompliant, leaving both student and teacher upset and neither of their goals accomplished.

Sharing Culture Across the Class: Dawan's Final Observation

Antoine entered the classroom a minute early today and walked directly over to Angela to share his piece of culture. Today is culture day and all the students were supposed to bring in something for show-and-tell that represented them as a companion to their culture projects. I couldn't hear what Antoine said to her, but he overflowed with excitement. When he finally sat down I asked him what he brought. Twice he told me and twice I was unable to make any connection between the word he said and any definition in my mind. Finally, sensing my disconnect, he started describing it as "dough that you cut up with some powdered sugar on top of it." Whatever it was, it sounded delicious. He told me he had stayed up until 2:00 A.M. making it because he had forgotten about the assignment. I was impressed.

Class began and Angela instructed the class to take 10 minutes to write about why they each brought what they brought and what "piece of you" was represented by their item. As she issued this invitation I heard Antoine say to himself, "What if you just brought it because you just brought it?" But as Angela asked the class, "Does that make sense?" Antoine replied with "I guess so."

The students continued writing. As they finally wrapped up their rationale statements, Angela presented the class with multiple options for sharing their poems, which were another element of their culture projects. She invited the class to decide as a group how they wanted to begin the sharing. The whole class erupted in a flurry of voices, but after the class vote, open mic won. Angela asked, "Who's going first?" and a student volunteered to share. At the conclusion of what he called his "free verse thing" the class clapped and snapped their fingers to show their approval. Another student had a turn and then Antoine spoke up.

"I'm gonna go to get it over with," he began. "My poem called 'Pain.'" The class listened intently and as he finished many students commented with phrases like "beautiful" and "nice job" along with the chorus of snaps. A few more students shared their poems and then Antoine spoke up again. "I'll go, I got another one," he shouted. But then he got self-conscious. "Oh, wait. She can go," he said, and drew back. The girl he yielded the floor to shared her poem and thanked everyone for listening.

The final few students shared their writing and everyone is obviously pleased with their work. As they got ready to transition to sharing another element of their culture projects, there was some side chatter going on. Antoine spoke up first; referring to himself in the third person, he announced,, "Antoine brought beignets!"

Everyone laughed and Angela smiled and invited him to come up to the front of the class and tell the class about them. Antoine told her, "I got nothing to tell. They be little French things. They some dough with some flour." He explained that what he called "ben gays" were actually beignets, a dessert particular to New Orleans. He talked briefly about how his family used to make them all the time and how everyone ate them back home. It got quiet for a moment and Angela asked him, "Why are they important to you?" Antoine says, "They're really not, they're just delicious. We just make them."

Angela realized she wasn't going to get much more discussion out of him and Antoine passed out his beignets as a Korean student in the class began to talk about what he brought to share. As Angela explained to the rest of the class the concept of "show-and-tell," Antoine reached my side of the room with his beignets and asked one of his classmates, "Are they good? No, for real? Are they good? It's my first time ever making them." Then, as he reached me he asked, "Did you want one?" I replied, "Yes. Definitely."

Antoine was proud of his beignets. He carried the box around and made sure the rest of the class got more. The class started making requests for orders and then telling him to make them softer. "It's my first time making them!" he replied. He was in front as a boy shared about his cross-country medals. Antoine sat in the director's chair up front. He was listening, involved, and not taking over the class, but definitely interested in being on the front lines of the action.

As the rest of the class finished sharing, Angela said that she was proud of them for sharing and what a great risk they took and how she appreciated the things they brought. Someone yelled, "We love you, Miss Dean!" and a few others echoed the sentiment. Then they started clapping really loud and long, just to keep it from being too awkward and sentimental. Someone yelled, "Thank you, everybody" and "especially . . . for the beignets." Finally the bell rang and they left.

I sat and watched the class that day, interested in the way the scene played out. Angela had mentioned feeling nervous that students wouldn't participate. I watched the kids come in that day and there were only three who had brought anything, from what I could see, to share. But the positive response Antoine received from the class (in addition to the fact there was an edible component) made it easy for others to share. bell hooks (2009) explained, "Sharing experiences . . . in the classroom helps establish communal commitment to learning. These narrative moments usually are the space where the assumption that we share a common class background and perspective is disrupted" (p. 139). Angela took the risk and called out to the class, inviting them to participate in a communal sharing experience. The class's response opened up the risk taking and some serious sharing took place after that. The tone of the class shifted, and a lot of discussions emerged that might not have been approached days before. Ultimately the singular calls and responses spread out across the context of the class through-out the year made all the difference in creating a space where these kinds of activities could be successful. In Antoine's case in particular, these dialogues helped him become invested in the class and find relevance in the curriculum.

You Don't Hear Me: Angela's Reflections on a Class Hour

Finally, April arrived and we were studying *Lord of the Flies* (Golding, 1954). The students in my first-period class were uproarious, making predictions about what would come of the boys on the island. The boarding school, English-accented, ragtag group of boys struggling to survive in the midst of nuclear fallout and what could very well be the end of their world as they knew it have captivated all of them, even Antoine. Golding's writing, with its long narrative descriptions that meander and distract most adolescent readers, has only made their experiences with the book more enticing. They are at the height of the conflict in the book where the boys' society is breaking down and splitting apart. Jack has gone completely savage and Ralph is left holding the sun-bleached conch. The students begged me to tell them if their predictions were correct. They wanted validation.

In the middle of them all was Antoine, the most vocal. On the edge of his seat, he vied for my attention. I wouldn't budge. I wouldn't tell them what came next. I asked them a few questions and as the room shouted out their replies, I picked up a few voices in the cacophony. From a few of their answers, I probed further, restating what the student shared and using his or her name to recognize that student's contribution. After a few questions, Antoine had it.

He said, "You don't hear me."

It was an accusation.

At this point in our relationship and in his engagement with academics, it wasn't enough for him to be part of the larger classroom and to have his voice add to their ideas. He called out again and again, just like the others, but I hadn't heard him.

"You don't hear me."

It stung.

I called, he responded, and I didn't use one of his responses to help drive the classroom forward in the discussion. He wanted validation for his ideas from me. He wanted me to see him, to hear him, to recognize him and to be acutely aware of the power of our interaction. And all of a sudden I did hear him, I did see him, but it was too late. Frustrated, yet lighthearted, he continued to grumble, moved back to his original seat, and started to pack up his things.

It was then that I realized that he wanted *me* to answer *his* call, only I hadn't paid attention to the signals of his calling out to me. As he turned away from the class, as he turned away from me, I understood that in this case he wanted a reciprocal participatory relationship. In the mix of students, it was enough for me that he was responding along with the rest of the kids.

What I didn't realize is that in his responding, he was also calling out to me. His calls fell flat when I would select a classmate's ideas, the same ideas as his own, to build upon. In the exchange, he was doing all the giving and he wanted me to return. Since I did not hear him, as he wanted me to hear him, he withdrew from the group. The tension of the give-and-take, the call-and-response, in this particular exchange is subtle. Antoine recognized my call and was engaged in ways that met my expectations.

I had failed to meet his.

IMPLICATIONS OF CALL-AND-RESPONSE: AN INVITATION FOR TEACHERS TO DIALOGUE

When the year began, Antoine chose to sit in the farthest reaches of the room, but over the course of first semester he would sometimes sit within the main section of desks if a student who normally sat there was out. Reading *Oedipus* started to draw him in and he wanted to be physically closer to the rest of the class. Then at some point during *Bronx Masquerade* (Grimes, 2002) he chose to claim a seat as close to the main section of desks as he could be and stayed there for the remainder of the year. When we shared our culture projects, he volunteered to share his when no one else raised his or her hand. His movement into the larger classroom community was a slow and sometimes subtle process. It was not all in one direction, but more of a roller coaster of highs and lows. There have been days where he clearly did not want to engage with anyone in the room, much less Angela, and days like when he came in beaming about his hard work making the class beignets.

What does this picture of Antoine, Angela, and their experiences offer all of us as educators? As critical educators we must strive to create spaces where we call to students and where their calls to us receive a response—even when that might feel too risky or as though a teacher is giving up too much of his or her power or control over the content and interactions in the classroom. Moore and Cunningham (2006) remind us that "when educators share the belief that people are active decision makers in the course of their lives, students have opportunities to evolve a greater sense of personal agency" (p. 142). Evolving a greater sense of agency cannot be accomplished through simply "responding" or "answering" to a teacher's prompts and questions. Rather, a sense of agency evolves when the traditional interaction patterns in classrooms that rely more on monologues, directions, and compliance are disrupted by the open and creative possibilities of call-and-response. The back-and-forth dialogue invoked in call-and-response provides space for all partners in the interaction to practice their agency and participation in ways that won't be shut down or harshly judged. This was particularly true for Antione.

Reflecting across the year, Angela and Antoine, and on some level the whole class, worked to share across cultures and volunteered parts of their selves. Freire and Macedo (1987) explained that "it is impossible to . . . understand literacy . . . by divorcing the reading of the word from the reading of the world" (p. 49). If called upon, we couldn't nail it down to a particular activity, discussion, or routine that made Antoine open up and engage with his teacher or with the literacy activities of the class. The daily calls issued by Angela that invited her students to respond in multiple ways helped them realize over the course of the semester that this class was a place where they mattered, where Antoine mattered.

This roller coaster ride of calls and responses demonstrates how it is imperative for teachers and the larger school community to recognize participation and contributions that students make, even when these contributions might not initially be what the teacher envisions (González, Moll, & Amanti, 2005). The cultural understandings different students bring to class include differences in discourse and interactional styles (Delpit, 2009). As teachers, looking beyond our own cultural traditions and valuing the contributions each student makes will open up the dialogues in our classrooms in ways that honor all student voices. Traditionally marginalized students especially need teachers willing to enter into dialogue with them without making accusations and without jumping to conclusions.

Additionally, participation must be dialogic (Fecho, 2011). The give and take nature of dialogue situates it as a participatory exchange where the response of one individual is contingent on the words of the other—not already known and simply being played out as in a script for a play. If we, as teachers, are truly engaging in a dialogic manner with our students, we will continually reflect on our own participation as well, not just that of our students, as we willingly allow our students' ideas and words to shape us, just as we expect our words to shape their understandings.

Finally, it remains essential for teachers and schools to remember that although students may seem disengaged or withdrawn from school, the interactions we have with them still matter. A willingness to engage with and take advantage of moments of dialogue with even seemingly "nonparticipatory" students can help teachers initiate transactions with students who might traditionally sit in the silences of the school community.

Guiding Prompts

1. Notice how Angela and Dawan use snippets of classroom data and quotes and ideas from theory to develop their key idea: A "call-and-response" approach to teaching opens up an invitation for both the student and the teacher to be empowered and transformed in the classroom. How do you and your students use call-and-response patterns of dialogue in the classroom? What do you notice about the dynamics of the classroom and engagement of you and your students during these times?

2. When do you notice that the interaction pattern in your classroom is not call-and-response, but something closer to "telling" or "directing" students? How does this change the dynamics of the classroom and the engagement of you and your students?

3. In what ways is this chapter written as a "call-and-response" piece? How does that influence the way readers may engage with the chapter?

Writing Group Exercise

Think of a time when a student in your classroom might have taken a risk to "call" for your response but for whatever reason the call fell flat and you did not respond. Write the student's "call" to you in quotations, and then begin free writing by starting with one way you might have responding to the call. How might that dialogue have continued? What creative and unknown possibilities might have happened if the call hadn't fell flat? Remember, this is fiction, so be playful and have fun. Read it out loud to yourself and anyone else who will listen, and then when you are back in the classroom see if the writing and sharing helped you to prepare yourself to be more open to your students' calls. And of course, write about that too.

REFERENCES

Bakhtin, M. M. (1981). *The dialogic imagination* (C. Emerson & M. Holquist, Trans.). Austin: University of Texas Press.

Bakhtin, M. M. (1986). *Speech genres and other late essays* (V. W. McGee, Trans). Austin: University of Texas Press.

Bakhtin, M. M. (1993). *Towards a philosophy of the act* (V. Liapunov, Trans). Austin: University of Texas Press.

Delpit, L. (2009). Language diversity and learning. In A. Darder, M. Baltodano, & R. D. Torres (Eds.), *The critical pedagogy reader.* (pp. 324–337). New York, NY: Routledge.

Fecho, B. (2011). *Writing in the dialogical classroom: Students and teachers responding to the texts of their lives.* Urbana, IL: National Council of Teachers of English.

Foster, M. (2001). Pay leon, pay leon, paleontologist: Using call-and-response to facilitate language mastery and literacy acquisition among African American students. In S. J. Lanehart (Ed.), *Sociocultural and historical contexts of African American English* (pp. 281–298). Philadelphia, PA: John Benjamins.

Foster, M. (2002). Using call-and-response to facilitate language mastery and literacy acquisition among African American students. *Center for Applied Linguistics Digest Series 1.* Retrieved from http://www.cal.org/resources/digest/0204foster.html

Freire, P., & Macedo, D. (1987). *Literacy: Reading the word and the world.* Westport, CT: Bergin & Garvey.

Golding, W. (1954). *Lord of the flies.* New York, NY: Penguin.

González, N., Moll, L. C., & Amanti, C. (2005). *Funds of knowledge: Theorizing practices in households, communities, and classrooms.* Mahwah, NJ: Lawrence Erlbaum.

Grimes, N. (2002). *Bronx masquerade.* New York, NY: Penguin.

hooks, B. (2009). Confronting class in the classroom. In A. Darder, M. Baltodano, & R. D. Torres (Eds.), *The critical pedagogy reader* (pp. 135–141). New York, NY: Routledge.

Moore, D. W., & Cunningham, J. (2006). Adolescent agency and literacy. In D. E. Alvermann, K. A. Hinchman, D. W. Moore, S. F. Phelps, & D. R. Waff (Eds.), *Reconceptualizing the literacies in adolescents' lives* (2nd ed., pp. 129–144). Mahwah, NJ: Lawrence Erlbaum.

Myers, W.D. (2004). *Monster.* New York, NY: Amistad.

Rogers, R. (2004). Setting an agenda for critical discourse analysis of literate identities across contexts: Alignment and conflict. In R. Rogers (Ed.), *An introduction to critical discourse analysis in education* (pp. 51–78). Mahwah, NJ: Lawrence Erlbaum.

Yin, R. (2009). *Case study research: Design and methods.* Los Angeles, CA: Sage.

CHAPTER 8

On Writing Selves and Other Selves Out of Bindedness

Toward Beauty and Grace

Stephanie Jones

> Looking, like writing, is a kind of composing—a selecting and ignoring—a looking and not looking.
>
> Barbara Kamler, *Relocating the Personal: A Critical Writing Pedagogy*

Recently I had to face a difficult fact of my life. The very sight of a school, even a school I had never seen before, produced knots in my stomach and sped up my heart. This response was not good for someone who studies schools, prepares future teachers to work in schools, and spends a good deal of time with teachers talking about school.

I was certain my semi-successful career in education had come screeching to a halt. If I couldn't even *drive by* a school without becoming nauseated, how was I going to continue to *work in* schools and be even the least bit productive?

The knotting in my stomach was accumulated across many years of being in many schools and witnessing unconscionable things. In one classroom it was the announcement of 5th-grade students' state test scores in front of the class, causing enormous tears to flood down tough boys' cheeks as they realized they would not be promoted to 6th grade. No one was celebrating, not even those who had passed the test, but rather, every young student in that classroom had faces of sadness. Tears welled in my eyes too, and a knot twisted in my gut, and I knew I was in a place of pain and sorrow and resentment even as the teacher tried to create a celebratory event for those who would successfully move on to the next grade.

In other classrooms it would be teachers' threats to the children in the "top" 3rd-grade class that they would be sent to the "low" class because of their behavior. And in another classroom it was a teacher calling to me across the room, "See if *you* can do something with him, I'm not dealing with him today!" after she read a piece of writing produced by a 1st-grader who was supposed to have written a nonnarrative informational text but only included 4 of the 5 required "steps" in the process. In too many schools to count, bulletin boards in hallways advertising the upcoming state tests as if they were carnivals made me furious. Military music booming over loudspeakers during a week of "Testing Bootcamp" made me physically sick. Kindergarteners not allowed to use crayons during writing time . . . Prekindergarteners permitted to have only a 10-minute recess . . . a 1st-grader reported to the police.

A kindergartener handcuffed and taken away.

My chest tightens just composing that short list of events I know took place—writing down what I have seen when I have chosen to look, not documenting what was happening when I have chosen to turn away. My body literally pulls into itself, a folding filled with anger, shame, sadness, fear, hatred. Strong feelings for someone committed to public education, but this is one gift neoliberalism has generously shared with schools and the gift it has given me personally—a one-size-fits-all curriculum and accountability system that wraps its tentacles around expectations, values, language, practices, and what used to be called "education" inside the only institution in the United States that has claimed for decades to be the great equalizer and route to upward mobility. The intensity of testing and measuring and concepts such as time-on-task, coupled with the diminished goals of social-emotional and physical well-being for children and youth, would drive even the best intentioned teacher to do things she would not have done under different policy directives.

This is the very restricted, constraining, oppressive, or what I would call "binded" context, however, that makes the work the teacher-writers have done in this book even more remarkable than it might seem. They wouldn't want me to say that, of course, fearful as they are about anyone accusing them of acting like saviors; knights in shining armor; or superhero teachers who come in to save the poor, disenfranchised kid in the corner. Teachers—even remarkable, extraordinary teachers—are always in a bind this way. Perceptive ones know that critically oriented researchers and advocates of critical pedagogy would balk at any claim by a teacher to have done something exceptional with and for students—they know the metaphors potentially used to describe such presumed arrogance, all tied to their assumed privilege and blissful ignorance. And yet if teachers don't speak out as if they know something important about pedagogy and the intimate ways they work with marginalized students, they are assumed to not know what they are doing, assumed to be privileged White women who can't make a difference in their racially, ethnically, and socioeconomically diverse students' lives, assumed they need scripted curriculum and testing accountability.

Yes, this is a bind many teachers find themselves in. Damned if they do act as if they know a thing or two, and damned if they don't.

And it was a bind I found myself in too: Damned if I did go into schools, and damned if I didn't.

The power of writing, however—linking word to word, moving passages around, sitting alone quietly and letting your body go limp in memory of the good and bad and indifferent, letting your body push through the keys to show you the sense that has been made and not yet imagined, then mustering the courage to send that writing out to others who will talk to you—provides pathways out of binds trapping our minds and bodies. We write and realize we don't have a word good enough for the feltness of a lived experience, challenged by the stunted nature of language to account for the body and bodily. Or we realize we don't even know how something happened, or who did what, or that we wish we were a different person acting in a different way at that particular time, or that something that seemed so simple in the moment turns out to be infinitely complex, and intertwined with the word-making and sense-making.

We wonder if it's all fiction.

And perhaps it is—all fiction.

Bear with me here for a moment, readers, but imagine it is all fiction: the way we perceive students and colleagues and administrators, the choices we make in our classrooms, the idea that we are monolingual or bound by our personal histories, that testing is the most important way to measure human growth. If we can suspend, for even a moment, that these are "truths" and therefore solidified like cement—if we can imagine, for even a moment, that what we are creating in response to the events around us is all fiction, then it is *not yet truth*. And if it is not yet truth, our understanding of it is not yet unmovable, not yet set in stone, not yet commonsense. Indeed, if it is fiction we are creating in our interactions and reflections, then we can reclaim some control over what it is we produce.

If it is all fiction—the writing, the pedagogy, the moments we remember in the classroom and in the faculty lounge—then we get to position ourselves as the creative artist who can write, speak, act our ways out of the messes in which we find ourselves.

As teachers and writers and researchers we are summoned to attend to one thing and not the other—one person and not the other—one angle and not the other—one place and not the other. And once we are summoned (by a student, by a piece of literature, by a test, by an administrator, by an injustice) we submit to the journey of being taken somewhere unpredictable, somewhere that wasn't possible before we were summoned and wasn't possible before we permitted ourselves to be taken away (MacLure, 2012). As contributors to this book, we realize we have submitted ourselves as writers to be summoned by different people and things at different places and times. The task at hand, as we see it, is not to *understand* some already existing truth of the event in front of us or in our memory, but rather to turn away from the idea of true understanding and toward realizing the impossible. Being with students differently today from how we were yesterday opens up a new trajectory of possibility—something that may have seemed impossible in the past.

The still fictional, and thus, the still open and possible.

The making and remaking of things: events, places, interactions, feelings, words, and relationships through writing is simultaneously a making and remaking of ourselves. We come to something new, we think something different, we learn something about ourselves and that learning opens up a line of sight closed to us just yesterday.

Our looking, like writing, is never neutral, never an individual autonomous decision made through rational thought, grounded in objectivity and the fantasy of reason. Looking, like writing, is shaped by social and political contexts in which we live and crafted through our habits of attention and inattention—habits formed through power relations circulating in the material conditions of our lives and discourses in our society. Boler (1999) tells us that we learn *not* to see because of fears of what might be seen, and to learn to see *differently* takes a willingness to live with fear and ambiguity—of not knowing and uncertainty.

It might be only by chance—a chance massaged by the attention it takes to write—that the stories in this book have ended up as they are. They might have been about different students, different interactions, an infinite number of other moments that are too painful to attend to, or too shameful, or too embarrassing, or too mundane and seemingly boring. And then of course there is all the ignoring we do too, the turning away, the pretending not to have heard, the "forgetting" we sometimes do just to survive the day that might have made its way into these stories. The ways we move as teachers in pedagogical spaces and choose to take up moments that seem critical or interesting, without even noticing all the others that pass us by, are multiplied in our act of writing about those pedagogical spaces.

Classrooms are dynamic and fluid and pedagogy is incredibly messy; writing about pedagogy attempts to make some sense of the messiness. Even when we are oriented toward noticing things such as exclusion or marginalization or inequity, we miss more than we see. And sometimes, when we are lucky, writing about our work can help us see beyond our creative horizon.

In other words, the crafting and recrafting of stories about students and ourselves produces a new pedagogical space, one tailor made for the pedagogue who steps into the mess and attempts sense-making from many different angles through creative undoing of what we thought we had known and remaking something new. We learn from these experimental writing endeavors that help us "evolve beyond the fixities and limitations of the present moment" (Davies, 2011, p. 30) and inherently we are changed by them.

Our bodies feel different.

Our eyes and ears attune themselves to something anew.

Our relanguaging work provides new words and phrases we can use to disrupt harmful, sedimented ways of perceiving and responding.

We still look away, ignore, forget, but those are altered as well.

The writings in this book provided that pedagogical space for all of us. They are stories constructed from moments *not* missed—or narratives about some of those missed moments only realized much later in time, all rearranged with wild abandon. They come from a decision to select one student or parent and not another to focus on across a year, to label—even if only temporarily—as disenfranchised, and to commit to *doing something different* in an effort of regeneration between student and teacher, family and institution.

Indeed, the writing of these stories became our own assembled conditions for critical pedagogy (Chapter 1). We leaned over the edge of predictability and were open to what might emerge when we suspended what we thought we already knew; we suspended any tendency to create strong divisions of right/wrong or good/bad, and instead cultivated a morally ambiguous sense of self as we worked with one another; and in our writing we were committed to the aesthetic.

It is not by chance, then, that these stories are carefully crafted literary pieces that draw on a broad range of art-making through composition: poetry, prose, metaphor, voice. Most of the authors would say they began with jotting notes, writing personal reflections, documenting interactions and pedagogical decisionmaking. Then they worked and reworked that material, read to the group, and talked to one another, and we talked as a group about the kinds of stories we hoped to tell and how we wanted to tell them.

Presenting the children, youth, and families in the writing was of central concern. How do you describe a young man's hardships at home without using language that blames his mother for her struggles with economic instability and feelings of powerlessness? And how do you explore the depth of meaning of a little girl's story without exploiting her—again—in a way that benefits yourself? The language to which we have access constrains us, pushes us toward perpetuating broad and damaging fixed stories about certain students and families and communities by not providing acceptable alternatives. Care with every word—and every word not used—becomes the focus. Every sentence, every metaphor, every literary reference has the potential for being read from a perspective that would layer on assumptions about working-class and poor kids, "urban" kids, "at risk" kids, and "disengaged" parents. We aren't willing to breathe more life into those stories, so we had to reread and reconsider every aspect of our crafting, allow ourselves to get carried away from reality, knowing these are not only narratives being formed, but subjects that readers will encounter and construct in their own minds as they read.

And ideas they might take with them into the world to read things differently.

So we write with wild abandon, with a commitment to being carried away, to imagine beyond the real right now.

We write our way out of the binds that hold us into patterns of stunted language and narrow vision, and we breathe new life into what used to be fictional possibilities for both ourselves and our students.

In this way, our writing changes the world.

Not because it changes other people, but because it changes us, and we move through the world differently, speaking about the once impossible and living in the used-to-be-fiction. The way we perceive people, places, and events are forever changed and will likely change again with the assistance of remaking ourselves through tending to bodies and writing.

A teacher willing to be summoned by injustice is engaged in the kind of sludging-through-the-mud work that we can do together to reach outside the complexities and contradictions of the issues we face, and to commit to following those without trying to understand the "real"—trying instead to imagine the possibilities. What will matter to the people standing in front of us, walking next to us, averting their eyes from us, and to ourselves? What are the small but powerful things we can do in our material existence that can reestablish connections across humanity, across intellectual disciplines, across needs and desires?

Do we act within our presumably binded position and call the police to take away a 6-year-old child throwing a temper tantrum?

Do we publicly announce who will be promoted and retained as a result of test scores?

Do we humiliate a child because we are frustrated workers?

Or do we act with the courageous sense of ambiguity the teachers in this book perform of both knowing and not knowing at the same time? Kneeling next to a child, befriending a mother, offering a piece of literature, writing in a dialogue journal, committing to poetry, chasing down permanent records, and learning a new language are all presented as intimate moments of undoing what used to be.

More courageous acts—both tiny and grand—are still fictions waiting to be determined in future interactions, but our willingness to be carried away by them—through looking or not looking—presents us with infinite opportunities to write ourselves out of bindedness and toward beauty and grace in the complicated world of critical teaching not yet known.

REFERENCES

Boler, M. (1999). *Feeling power: Emotions and education.* New York, NY: Routledge.

Davies, B. (2011). An experiment in writing place. In M. Somerville, B. Davies, K. Power, S. Gannon, & P. de Carteret (Eds.), *Place pedagogy change.* Dordrecht, The Netherlands: Sense.

Kamler, B. (2001). *Relocating the personal: A critical writing pedagogy.* Albany: State University of New York Press.

MacLure, M. (2012, April). *Language and materiality in qualitative methodology.* Paper presented at the annual meeting of the American Educational Research Association, Vancouver, British Columbia.

Oral Inquiry Processes

Teacher Research from PhilWP to the Red Clay Writing Project

Bob Fecho

The high school teachers weren't making it easy for Judy Buchanan. It was the first summer institute of the Philadelphia Writing Project (PhilWP) and Judy, who would go on to become deputy director of the National Writing Project, was then an elementary teacher trying to explain the descriptive review process. Worse yet, she wanted the high school teachers gathered in a circle before her to give the process a try. She had an expectation that these English teachers, who were so fond of raising critique wherever they might find it, would ease off that stance and instead open themselves to a shared construction of the complexity of a single student. In the patient way that is her hallmark, Judy explained that a descriptive review was intended to view children from several facets of their lives, to gather multiple perspectives, to focus on description rather than evaluation, and to ensure that all voices were heard and considered. "Too controlling," someone said. "It doesn't feel natural." "It takes too long." We were having none of it.

I say *we*, because I was one of those high school teachers. I like to think that I was more accepting of the process than my colleagues. But I suspect Judy might tell you otherwise. She will also tell you that while a full-blown descriptive review never became an integral part of the work of PhilWP, the theories and assumptions that provided its structure did. Although I can't speak for my fellow teacher consultants from that summer institute, I do know that the concepts of attempting to describe, of finding ways for many voices to be included and heard, of seeking complexity in understanding what occurs in classrooms, and of believing that much can be learned by looking closely at one child have influenced both how I teach and how I research from that day forward.

As a member of the Teacher's Learning Cooperative (TLC) (Abu El-Haj, 2003), Judy had been immersed in what have become known as oral inquiry processes (Cochran-Smith & Lytle, 1993). This group of Philadelphia teachers who met on their own volition every Thursday during the school year were much influenced by ideas and practices from Vito Perone's North Dakota Study Group on Evaluation and Patricia Carini's Prospect School in Vermont. It was Judy's involvement in TLC that induced Susan Lytle, founding director of PhilWP, to invite her, along with Rhoda Kanevsky, to work with PhilWP teachers that first summer in 1986. It was this direct connection between TLC and PhilWP that enabled the implementation of oral inquiry processes in ways that still resonate with me today. Because when I sat back and gave consideration to what I, and all participants, gained through the process, I realized that the concerns raised during that first experience were dwarfed in comparison.

ORAL INQUIRY PROCESSES AND THE DESCRIPTIVE REVIEW

Oral inquiry processes is a large umbrella category for protocols that enable groups of participants—in this case, teachers—to co-construct meaning from a close exploration of common events, issues, policies, and lived experiences. The oral inquiry processes I most value are all figured by clear demarcations of turn taking so that no one voice dominates; mutually understood and accepted guidelines for proceeding; a focus on reflection, description, and connection; and means for valuing and recording all that gets shared within the group. Within such parameters, many variations of oral inquiry processes can flourish.

A descriptive review, as practiced by teachers of the Prospect School and TLC, is emblematic of all these features. I have participated in only a handful of descriptive reviews, but the ones in which I've participated have been powerful experiences. Imagine a group of concerned teachers—maybe 5, maybe 15—being asked to look closely at the work and behaviors of one child. If you read Margaret Himley and Pat Carini's book on descriptive reviews (2000), and I suggest you do, you'll be aware of words like *narrative, layering, observing,* and *attentiveness* being used over and over in their explanations of the process. The telling of a child's story from keenly observed multiple perspectives is intended to provide a layered and nuanced understanding of that child, of the teaching and learning that surrounds that child, and of the potential it all holds for other children and their teachers.

The descriptive reviews in which I have participated proceeded, for the most part, in the following manner. First, a teacher would have collected data on a child, using her observations, the observations of others, and archival data. That data would be collected and shared within five categories: physical presence and gesture, disposition and temperament, connections with other people, strong interests and preferences, and modes of thinking. To start the review, a person acting as chair reminded participants of the values of respect, inclusion, description, and confidentiality, as well as of the process in general. The presenting teacher then posed framing questions for the group and began sharing her story of the child, starting with the physical description. At the conclusion of her comments, and after any questions of clarification, participants in the circle suggested what stood out to them in this account, one participant after another going in order until all thoughts on the matter had been shared. At this point, the chair, having gathered and semi-organized the notes—a true learning process, that—gave a summary of the responses. On we would similarly go through the next four categories. At the end would come suggestions for working with the child—delivered in the same way as category responses—and a debriefing of the process itself.

CONFRONTING THE DOUBTS

Many first-time participants in a descriptive review find it a bit controlling. Most of us in current Western education are used to a more freewheeling, back-and-forth kind of discourse. Some racial, ethnic, socioeconomic class, and regional groups—for example, working-class African Americans or urban Northeasterners—have often been raised with discourses where response is more overlapping and turn taking more aggressively sought. For such groups and others, the first response to the process is a sense of artificiality and lifelessness. I certainly felt that way on my first go at the process. However, my response

now to that response is to give the process a chance. Having participated in subsequent descriptive reviews and many more adaptations
of that process, I have come to see the power and life within it. Because
no one voice or any one idea gets to dominate, because care is taken
to be inclusive and to withhold evaluation, and because the child is
portrayed as a multidimensional and complex being, the artificiality
of regulated turn taking soon disappears under the vitality of the co-
constructed understanding.

In addition, what might feel artificial at first soon becomes an accepted norm. That which we have not experienced frequently feels
alien and thus odd or less organic to us on first encounter. In *The Brothers Karamasov*, Dostoevsky (1922) described two adolescents watching
dogs greet each other, with the accompanying sniffing that occurs.
When one young man suggests it to be a funny habit, the other count-
ers, "If dogs could reason and criticize us, they'd be sure to find just
as much that would be funny to them, if not far more, in the social
relations of men, their masters" (p. 566). Later in the same discussion,
the second young man remarks how the first cold days of winter seem
much colder than later days when the temperature is even more se-
vere. In the first instance, he suggests, we are not used to the chill and
thus feel it more. But deeper into winter, because "everything is habit
with men, everything even in their social and political relations" (p.
567), we accept the frigid temperatures as the norm. So it is with oral
inquiry processes. The more I used variations of these protocols, the
more familiar they became, and the more relaxed and connected my
participation.

First-time participants also often express their doubt that focusing
on the experiences of one child will yield much of substance and con-
sequence. They worry that such exploration is too focused and local.
As Himley and Carini (2000) insisted, however, "The portrayal of the
child is the heart of the descriptive review" (p. 15). The mutual inquiry
of the participants is intended to "add dimension and depth to the
picture of the child" (p. 15). It is this multiple layering that imbues
the process with vitality and substance. Moreover, aside from providing the presenting teacher with a more developed and enhanced understanding of the child, all who participated gained greater insight
into their own classrooms and became more adept at paying careful
attention to the children who endeavored to learn there. Returning to
the words of Himley and Carini (2000), "The habit of observing and
describing and pooling our knowledge and perspectives on a child

made us disciplined students of childhood" (p. 16). And it is from such engagement that teacher practice remains in process.

ADAPTING ORAL INQUIRY PROCESSES

A mantra I share with preservice and inservice teachers is *adapt, don't adopt*. What I mean by that is to call teaching programs, cool activities, innovative approaches, and the like into question and, if you are still willing to implement them in your classroom, *adapt* them to your context rather than *adopting* them wholesale. All learning and meaning is contingent on context and so savvy teachers examine the theories and assumptions that underpin a teaching approach. Having done so, they can then enact some version of that approach that remains true to the foundations that are at its core, but also responsive to local context.

Such has been my experience with oral inquiry processes. As much as I admire the Prospect School and TLC teachers for their commitment to descriptive review, I know that I have rarely been able to devote that much time to the exploration. Reviews I have been partner to have all taken 90 minutes or more to complete and, given the seriousness of the intent, one shouldn't expect them to be rushed. If the idea is to gather multiple perspectives on a wide description of the child, the process needs all the time it takes.

To me, what sits at the core of descriptive review and other oral inquiry process is a stated focus, the posing of framing questions, the seeking of multiple perspectives, a withholding of evaluation, a procedure of inclusion, and a means for making meaning. Armed with these assumptions, I have created a variety of processes for both teaching and research that have reflected these values. For example, the small learning community where I taught high school used a variation when we felt a student was struggling. We would invite all of that student's teachers, his counselor, his adult guardians, and other advocates—along with the student—to a session where we sat around a conference table. After briefly framing why we felt a need for having the meeting, we would start the first of three rounds, each round driven by the following sequence of questions: (1) What strengths does this student bring to school? (2) What struggles is this student having in school? and (3) What individual responsibilities can we all take for using this student's strengths to work through the struggles? Then, just as in a descriptive review, all in turn, including the student, would respond to each question. Notes would be taken and summarized at the end of each round. Finally, the meeting would end with all at the table having clear responsibility for some aspect of moving forward.

Although not a complete descriptive review, this process honored the core strengths of that more encompassing exploration. Furthermore, it fit the context and needs of this group of teachers, parents, and students. It was often illuminating for the teacher who requested the session to see the student—one who perhaps she was finding it hard to see in anything but negative terms—in positive ways, and to, in fact, add to that positive description. Gaining multiple perspectives and honoring the perspectives of all at the table positioned the session more as a mutual support effort than a punitive scapegoating. It was also key that parents, teachers, and the student were all expected to take part in the co-constructed plan for moving ahead. Rather than all responsibility being heaped on the student, responsibility was shared. And, by focusing on the needs of one child, we came away with a more complex understanding of the needs of other children.

THE RED CLAY TEACHER INQUIRY COMMUNITY ADAPTATION

As the Red Clay Writing Project TIC group began to imagine ways that it would work together, the idea of doing some variation of an oral inquiry process made sense. Given that the teachers were all working at different schools and grade levels, we needed some cohesive way to delve into those situations and to do it in ways that invited a range of perspectives. We felt the latter point was especially necessary in order to help each teacher gain some distance and other ways of seeing their classrooms.

To this end, we negotiated the following oral inquiry process. Each teacher would write weekly journal responses on the project wiki, an interactive website that acted as a repository for all data collected in the project. At some point in the year, each teacher selected a significant transaction she had previously written about in the wiki journal and fleshed it out to a two- to four-page narrative. Meeting one Saturday morning a month, we then subjected the narratives to a variation of an oral inquiry process, usually doing one or two narratives per session.

The author of the narrative would begin by reading it aloud, although she could opt to have us read to ourselves or have someone else read it aloud. After the reading, the other participants would jot notes on the three default questions listed below.

Q1: What stood out for you in this text? Why?
Q2: What issues about critical pedagogy and learners marginalized by school does this text raise? Why?
Q3: What connections/associations to your own experience/ writing did you make to the text? Why?

On any given Saturday, the presenting teacher could tailor the questions to her needs, but that rarely occurred. With the presenting teacher as note taker, the other participants would address the first question, each giving one response in turn. We continued sharing until each of us had exhausted all responses. At that point, the author summarized the responses from her notes. Questions 2 and 3 were handled in a similar manner. We then finished the session with an open discussion of any lingering ideas, clarifications, or comments on the process.

Again, the intent was to honor the core assumptions of descriptive reviews and other oral inquiry processes while also creating a way of working that more closely fit the needs of this group. The rich and involving insights, inspired by equally rich and involving classroom narratives, provided the group members with much to contemplate as they sought to generate greater understanding of students who were being swept into the dusty corners of the schoolyard. Gradually, as we completed a few of these sessions, the questions and doubts that had been raised before we began to share our work faded into the background as the power of diverse and thoughtful perspectives made itself known. I found myself wishing that Judy could see me now.

REFERENCES

Abu El-Haj, T. (2003). Practicing for equity from the standpoint of the particular: Exploring the work of one urban teacher network. *Teachers College Record, 105*(5), 817–845.

Cochran-Smith, M., & Lytle, S. (1993). *Teacher research and knowledge.* New York, NY: Teachers College Press.

Dostoevsky, F. (1922). *The brothers Karamasov.* New York, NY: Macmillan.

Himley, M., with Carini, P. (2000). *From another angle: Children's strengths and school standards.* New York, NY: Teachers College Press.

Some of Our Favorite Readings on Teacher Research

Blackburn, M. V., Clark, C. T., Kenney, L. M., & Smith, J. L. (2009). *Acting out! Combating homophobia through teacher activism.* New York, NY: Teachers College Press.

Boran, S., & Comber, B. (2001). *Critiquing whole language and classroom inquiry.* Urbana, IL: National Council of Teachers of English.

Campano, G. (2007). Immigrant students and literacy: Reading, writing, and remembering. New York, NY: Teachers College Press.

Cochran-Smith, M., & Lytle, S. L. (1993). *Inside/outside: Teacher research and knowledge.* New York, NY: Teachers College Press.

Cochran-Smith, M., & Lytle, S. (2009). *Inquiry as stance: Practitioner research for the next generation.* New York, NY: Teachers College Press.

Compton-Lilly, C. (2002). *Reading families: The literate lives of urban children.* New York, NY: Teachers College Press.

Cowhey, M. (2006). *Black ants and Buddhists.* Portland, ME: Stenhouse.

Darling-Hammond, L. (1996). The quiet revolution: Rethinking teacher development. *Educational Leadership, 53*(6), 4–10.

Falk, B., & Blumenreich, M. (2005). *The power of questions: A guide to teacher and student research.* Portsmouth, NH: Heinemann.

Fecho, B. (2003). *Is this English? Race, language, and culture in the classroom.* New York, NY: Teachers College Press.

Frank, C., Green, J. L., & Dixon, C. N. (1999). *Ethnographic eyes: A teacher's guide to classroom observation.* Portsmouth, NH: Heinemann.

Gallas, K. (1997). *Sometimes I can be anything: Power, gender, and identity in a primary classroom.* New York, NY: Teachers College Press.

Hankins, K. (2003). *Teaching through the storm: A journal of hope.* New York, NY: Teachers College Press.

Hicks, D. (2013). *The road out: A teacher's odyssey in poor America.* Berkeley: University of California Press.

Himley, M., & Carini, P. F. (2000). *From another angle: Children's strengths and school standards.* New York, NY: Teachers College Press.

Hubbard, R. S., & Power, B. M. (1993). *The art of classroom inquiry.* Portsmouth, NH: Heinemann,.

Jones, S. (2006). *Girls, social class, and literacy: What teachers can do to make a difference.* Portsmouth, NH: Heinemann.

Lieberman, A. (1996). Creating Intentional Learning Communities. *Educational Leadership, 54*(3), 51–55.

Morrell, E. (2004). *Becoming critical researchers.* New York, NY: Peter Lang.

Rogers, R., Kramer, M. A., Mosley, M., & the Literacy for Social Justice Teacher Research Group (2009). *Designing socially just learning communities: Critical literacy education across the lifespan.* New York, NY: Routledge.

Vasquez, V. M. (2004). *Negotiating critical literacies with young children.* Mahwah, NJ: Lawrence Erlbaum.

Some of Our Favorite Readings on Writing

Brande, D. (1981). *Becoming a writer*. New York, NY: Tarcher.

Cofer, J. O. (2000). *Woman in front of the sun: On becoming a writer*. Athens: University of Georgia Press.

Cover, J. O. (2012). *Lessons from a writer's life: Readings and resources for teachers and students*. Portsmouth, NH: Heinemann.

Goldberg, N. (1994). *Long quiet highway: Waking up in America*. New York, NY: Bantam.

Goldberg, N. (2010). *Writing down the bones: Freeing the writer within*. Boston, MA: Shambhala.

Kamler, B. (2001). *Relocating the personal: A critical writing pedagogy*. Albany: State University of New York Press.

Kidder, T., & Todd, R. (2013). *Good prose: The art of non-fiction*. New York, NY: Random House.

King, S. (2000). *On writing*. New York, NY: Scribner.

Lamott, A. (1995). *Bird by bird: Some instructions on writing and life*. New York, NY: Anchor.

Nelson, G. L. (2004). *Writing and being: Embracing your life through creative journaling*. Novato, CA: New World Library.

Prose, F. (2007). *Reading like a writer: A guide for people who love books and for those who want to write them*. New York, NY: Harper Perennial.

About the Editor and Contributors

Stephanie Jones is associate professor in the Department of Educational Theory and Practice at the University of Georgia. Stephanie participated in the Ohio Writing Project when she was a classroom teacher and has been codirecting the Red Clay Writing Project since 2008. She is author of many publications exploring critical literacies, social class, gender, childhood, families, and teacher education, including *Girls, Social Class, and Literacy: What Teachers Can Do to Make a Difference* and *The Reading Turn-Around: A Five-Part Framework for Differentiated Instruction.*

Dawan Coombs is assistant professor in the Department of English at Brigham Young University.

Angela Dean is a high school English teacher and active Red Clay Writing Project teacher consultant who regularly attends and presents at the National Writing Project annual meeting and the National Council of Teachers of English conference.

Bob Fecho is professor of language and literacy education at the University of Georgia, where he has codirected the Red Clay Writing Project since 2003. He has long been committed to engaging in and supporting teacher-research and is author of numerous articles and books, including his most recent, *Teaching for the Students: Habits of Heart, Mind, and Practice in the Engaged Classroom.*

Allisa Hall completed the Red Clay Writing Project's Summer Institute in 2007. She has since devoted her spare time to writing and learning through National Writing Project. She currently serves as state coordinator for the six writing project sites in Georgia and advocates for NWP each spring in Washington, DC. She is part of the Holocaust Educator Network (HEN) and incorporates Holocaust literature study into her

10th-grade world literature classes. She is a part-time doctoral student in UGA's Department of Language and Literacy Education and a full-time teacher and mother. Her poems have been published in *English Journal*.

Daphne M. Hall is a veteran educator devoted to meeting the needs of English language learners in schools and communities.

Becky Hasty is a veteran high school English teacher in rural Georgia. She enjoys graphic novels, vampire series, and making connections with kids through nontraditional literature.

Jennifer McCreight is assistant professor at Hiram College, where she teaches literacy methods courses in the early childhood education certification program. Her research and teaching interests focus on early childhood literacy and family-community relations.

Jaye Thiel is a doctoral candidate in the Department of Language and Literacy Education at the University of Georgia, where she teaches undergraduate courses in literacy and works with teachers in the Red Clay Writing Project. Her research interests center on social class, education, and society; philosophy; and the material-discursive production of a phenomenon she calls "muchness" for working-class people of all ages.

Index